What is the Romani language?

The Interface Collection, coordinated and developed by the Gypsy Research Centre at the Université René Descartes, Paris, is published with the support of the European Commission.

Some Collection titles receive Council of Europe support for distribution in Central and Eastern Europe.

The views expressed in this work are the author's, and do not necessarily reflect those of the publisher nor of the Gypsy Research Centre or its research groups (historians, linguists, education specialists and so on).

Director of the Collection: Jean-Pierre Liégeois
Editorial assistant: Astrid Thorn Hillig

Cover design by Catherine Liégeois based on a painting by Ferdinand Koçi
DTP: Frédérique Vilain, GD-Infographie

© 2000
Centre de recherches tsiganes (Gypsy Research Centre) and
University of Hertfordshire Press
University of Hertfordshire
College Lane
Hatfield
Hertfordshire
AL10 9AB - UK

Tel. +44 1707 284654
Fax. +44 1707 284666

ISBN: 1 902806 06 9
Published: 2000

What is the Romani language?

Written by Peter Bakker, Milena Hübschmannová,
Valdemar Kalinin, Donald Kenrick, Hristo Kyuchukov,
Yaron Matras and Giulio Soravia

Edited by Peter Bakker and Hristo Kyuchukov

Centre de recherches tsiganes
University of Hertfordshire Press

This title is part of a series dealing with school provision and related matters, conceived in the framework of the activities of the Gypsy Research Centre-based *European working Group on Gypsy and Traveller Education*. This series is coodinated by **Hristo Kyuchukov**, a member of that Group.

Peter Bakker is a linguist working at the University of Aarhus. His main field of research is languages in contact. His interests include Pidgins, Creoles, Native American Indian languages and Romani.

Milena Hübschmannová works at Charles University in Prague in a department devoted to Romani studies. She has published widely on Roma and Romani, among others text collections, a dictionary and scientific essays.

Valdemar Kalinin is a Bible translator, poet and interpreter from Belarus residing in London. Romani is his first language. His publications include religious works, poetry and essays on Roma and Romani.

Donald Kenrick is a linguist from London. He has worked with adult education and language throughout his life. He has published widely on the Romani language and Roma, especially their fate during the Second World War.

Hristo Kyuchukov is a psycholinguist from Bulgaria. His research fields include child language and language contact. Languages of interest include Turkish and Romani, both of which are his native languages.

Yaron Matras is a linguist working at the University of Manchester, England. His main fields of research and publications are linguistic typology, language contact and discourse. His language interests include Kurdish, German dialects, Arabic, Turkish and Romani.

Giulio Soravia is a linguist working at the University of Bologna. His fields of research are grammar and descriptive linguistics. His language interests include Arabic, Somali, Indonesian and Romani. He has published especially on Romani in Italy.

Contents

Preface

This book deals with the Romani language, the language of the Gypsies or Roma. It is not intended for scholars, but for all those who have an interest in the language. These may be Roma, administrators, teachers, pupils, etc.

It is the first of three volumes on the language, all designed for educational purposes. This volume introduces the language of a people who are surrounded with so much mystification, misunderstanding and mistreatment. Whereas this book is of a general nature, the second volume will contain more detailed information on Romani dialects, dialect groupings and country-specific information. The third will consist of a tape, with a selection of stories in Romani from various parts of the world, so that readers can also hear the living language together with texts. They will all be published in the Instructional Series of the Interface Collection.

This book is the collective work of a number of people. The following persons, in alphabetical order, were involved in the planning of the contents: Peter Bakker, Dieter Halwachs, Mozes Heinschink, Milena Hübschmannová, Donald Kenrick, Hristo Kyuchukov, Jean-Pierre Liégeois, Yaron Matras, and Giulio Soravia. Of these, Peter Bakker, Milena Hübschmannová, Donald Kenrick, Hristo Kyuchukov, Yaron Matras and Giulio Soravia wrote parts of the different chapters. Valdemar Kalinin also contributed to the text. Most of the chapters were written jointly by several people; Yaron Matras wrote chapters 1 and 8. The authors have a variety of experience with Romani, and this is also reflected in the geographical span of this book. A number of persons also made critical comments which have been incorporated in the book, including Christina MacDonald, Sinéad ní Shuinéar. Peter Bakker and Donald Kenrick edited the final text. Sebastian Adorján Dyhr assisted with the conversion of files and provided other technical support. Hristo Kyuchukov is the editor of the Didactic Series. Illustrations were provided by Peter Bakker, Milena Hübschmannová, Hristo Kyuchukov, Remmelt Lukkien and the Centre de recherches tsiganes. The proverbs were selected by Hristo Kyuchukov and Peter Bakker from the collections of Milena Hübschmannová and Marcel Courtiade.

In this book we have chosen to use headings which summarise short sections to enable the reader to select those passages in which he or she is most interested. The book can also be read from cover to cover – and of course we hope that many readers will do that.

Introduction

In this introductory chapter we will discuss some of the most important terms relating to the Gypsies and their language, as they are used in this book.

Roma, Sinti, Gypsies, Zigeuner, Gitanos and Gadže

Gypsies are known by many names. Roma and Sinti are two names that Gypsies use for themselves. Outsiders use other names, such as Zigeuner, Gitan, Tsigane, Gypsy, but the names Roma (in Germany) and Sinti are to be preferred. In this book, the terms "Roma" and "Romani" are employed rather than "Gypsies". Nevertheless, we sometimes use the last word, especially when we want to generalise about several groups of Romani speakers who do not all call themselves "Roma". The term "Gypsy" and "Gypsies" should otherwise be avoided, since many Roma consider it an unpleasant word. Our employment of terms other than "Roma" is not meant to be belittling or degrading.

Just as in English the word "Gypsy" refers to a variety of different groups of people, the Roma have one word to denote all non-Roma. This word is "Gadže", and we will occasionally use this term in the book. Even though some Roma consider it a negative term, we use it since it covers a wide range of somewhat distinct population groups in Europe.

What is the difference between Roma, Gypsies and Travellers?

The word "Gypsies" is sometimes used for all people who live in caravans or lead a travelling life. The same word is used for those people who speak a language of their own and are more like an ethnic minority group. These people speak a language they call "Romani" or "Romanes" in their own tongue. Almost all of them call themselves "Roma". Even though there is a certain overlap between the people who live in caravans and people who belong to this ethnic group, they must be clearly distinguished. In fact, the vast majority of the people who speak Romani are not living in caravans, wagons or tents, and have not done so for many centuries.

"Roma" is the term by which most of those people who speak Romani call themselves. "Roma" is the plural form of the word "Rom"; where English uses an -s-ending (human, humans), Romani often uses an -a-ending to denote that more than one person or thing is involved. Some people prefer an English ending for the word, and they say "Roms", but we use "Roma", following the most common usage. Some groups in western Europe may use other terms for themselves, such as *Kalo, Sinti, Manuš, Romanichal* or *Romano*. These belong historically to the Roma people, as they speak varieties of the same language, and most call their language *Romanes* as well.

The term "Travellers" is used for (and by) people who have lived in caravans for generations. They often form tightly knit groups. There are groups like these in many countries. In contrast to "Gypsies", the Travellers mostly do not have a language of their own, but they often use a set of words only known to them.

This book is not about the language of "Travellers". This book deals with the Romani language. It is restricted to the language called "Romani" used by the ethnic group called "Gypsies" by outsiders.

Is it Roma or Rroma, and Romani or Rromani?

The spellings Roma and Rroma for the people, and Romani and Rromani for the language are all used. Both are correct. Strictly speaking, the spelling with double <rr> is better, since many dialects of Romani have two distinct r-sounds which are distinguished by spelling the first with one <r> and the second with double <rr>. Roma and Romani are more common, and therefore we use these spellings.

Roma and Sinti

In some publications, one can see the phrase "Roma and Sinti". What does that mean? Different groups of Gypsies call themselves by other names. These are two of them. In areas where both are present in significant numbers, the Gypsies and many journalists use this combined name. The Sinti have been present in western Europe since the 15th century, whereas most Roma came from south-eastern Europe in the 19th and 20th century. Both speak distinct varieties of the same language, which both Roma and Sinti call Romanes.

Are all Roma (Gypsies) the same?

There is a slogan which can be heard by members of nearly all Romani groups in their various dialects: *sem Roma sam, isem Roma st'am, hem Roma sam* "we of course are Roma!" This phrase expresses a feeling and awareness of the basic unity and identity of what the Roma call *Romipen, Romanipen* or *Romimo* "Romaniness, Romani identity, Romani culture".

However, there is another slogan which is *Roma nane jekh*. This means "Roma are not all the same". This shows that Roma differ not only as individuals, but also from group to group. This will also become clear in this book. Romani shows dialect differences, but it is clearly one and the same language.

Romani is not the same
as Romanian and not a Romance language

The names Roma and Romani resemble 'Romania', the name of a country. The origin of the names are completely different, and they have nothing to do with one another. The name of the country Romania and their language Romanian originate from Rome and Romans, and dates from the time when the Romans conquered part of the Balkans. Also the name of the Italian capital Rome or Roma has nothing to do with the name of the Roma. The similarity is pure coincidence.

Similarly the name "Romance" has nothing to do with the stem used in "Romani". Languages which descend from Latin are called the Romance languages. This groups includes Spanish, French, Italian, Portuguese and Romanian, but *not* Romani. Romani is *not* a Romance language, and it is *not* a dialect of Romanian.

Para-Romani

Para-Romani is a term that linguists have proposed to refer to a number of languages which share their vocabulary with Romani, but not the grammatical system. Gypsies and descendants of them in Britain, Norway, Sweden, Spain and Portugal speak such varieties. The speakers call the language usually Calo, Romanes or Romano, i.e. the same name as Romani speakers call it. Nevertheless, these must be considered different languages.

The Romani used in this book

Several people have co-operated in the production of this book. No attempt has been made to standardise the spelling of the Romani words. Instead, we have decided to preserve the flavour of the diversity of the language. We are confident that the varieties are close enough, so that most of the examples will be understood by a majority of the Romani speakers in the world.

Spelling used

Our spellings use a number of letters which are common in written Romani but which may be unfamiliar to the readers. These are:

c   Like English <ts>, e.g. 'Betsy';

č   Like English <ch>, e.g. 'church' or 'chalk';

čh   Like English <ch>, followed by an h-sound, e.g. 'church holiday';

dž   Like English <j>, e.g. 'jaw';

j   Like German <j> or English <y>, e.g. English 'year';

kh   Like English <k>, followed by an h-sound, e.g. 'bank holiday';

ň, ñ   Like <ñ> in Spanish mañana, or Italian <gn> in 'lasagna';

ph   Like English <p>, followed by an h-sound, e.g. 'uphold';

š   Like English <sh>, e.g. 'show', 'sheet';

th   Like English <t>, followed by an h-sound, e.g. 'boat house';

x   Like <ch> in German, Polish or Czech, or like in Scottish 'loch';

z   Like English <z>, e.g. in 'zone';

ž   Like French <j> or the sound written 's' in English 'measure' or 'treasure';

'   This symbol indicates that the preceding consonant combines with a j-sound. The 'ñ' sound is an example. It could also be written <n'>.
It is also used sometimes to mark an omitted vowel, e.g. s'oda = so oda;

a   Roughly like English <a> in 'master' or <u> in 'gun';

o   Like English <o> in 'go'; or like <o> in 'pot';

e   Like English <e> in 'pet' or roughly as <ay> in 'day';

i   Roughly like English <i> in 'pin' or <y> in 'happy' or <ea> in 'sea';

u   Like <u> in English 'pull' or <oo> in 'too'.

The name of the language is sometimes spelled Romani, sometimes Romany. Romany is often used in English, but we use the word Romani for the language, like Hindi, Punjabi, etc. This also reflects international usage, and the spelling systems designed for Romani.

I. Origins of Romani

This chapter deals with the historical question of where the Roma came from, and how we can know this. In this, language plays an important role, as it is primarily through the language that the origin of the Roma has been established. The chapter also discusses some groups which may or may not be related to the Roma.

Where did the Roma come from?

We do not know exactly when the first Roma arrived in Europe. Scholars now assume that Roma had settled in large numbers in south-eastern Europe (the Byzantine Empire) sometime between the 10th and 13th centuries. From the fourteenth century onwards, Roma began arriving in Central and Western Europe. This led scholars to seek an answer to the question of the origin of the "Gypsies". From their foreign language and customs, their way of dress and dark complexion, and their sudden arrival in small groups it was clear that this was a population of immigrants from a distinct and distant region. When questioned about this, the people themselves were vague about their origin. Some claimed to be from "Little Egypt" or even "India", others from "Greece". From the first country the name "Gypsy" was derived, as were Spanish Gitano, Basque Ijito and some other names given to the Romanies. Speculations about their origin prevailed until the second half of the 18th century. It has since been accepted that the language spoken by the Roma reflects their origin in India.

European recognition
of the Indian origin of the Romani language

Initially, researchers compiled word lists and compared them with various languages in an attempt to find the language that is closest to Romani. This, they conjectured, would provide evidence as to which nation is closest to them and so which might be the original homeland from which they emigrated to Europe. But the task was not to be done on the basis of words alone, since Romani, like all other languages, includes words that have been borrowed. Some superficial similarities with a series of languages appeared and no definite conclusions could be drawn. Scholars compared Romani with all the European languages and also with Ethiopian, languages of Egypt like Arabic, Coptic and Old Egyptian, but all in vain. Some people even thought the language was made up by the Roma.

Johann Rüdiger showed in 1782 that the similarities between Romani and Hindustani were so great, that these languages must come from the same source. These lines from Rüdiger's study, first in Romani, then in Hindustani and then in German, mean roughly: "Your brother sneezes, your sister sleeps, your father is awake, he does not eat and drinks little. The nose is the middle of the face. We have two feet..."

It was only toward the end of the eighteenth century that a group of scholars in England, Germany and Russia, who had been exchanging their views on the origin of the Gypsies based on samples of their language, became more and more convinced that the similarities with Indic languages (that is, languages spoken in India) were more systematic than those with any other language group. This conclusion was possible because grammar books and lists of words from languages spoken in India became available in the 18th century. The idea of an Indian origin was tested by the German scholar Johann Rüdiger. A Romani woman residing in Germany translated entire sentences into the language for him. They compared not only the words but also the grammatical structure with that of Hindustani or Hindi-Urdu, the main language of India. Rüdiger published the results of his study in 1782, showing that the two languages were similar as only two related languages can be. Languages are said to be related if they descend from a common ancestor language. For example, English is fairly closely related to German and less closely with French. Rüdiger concluded that Romani was an Indic language. Its speakers had left India and had since absorbed various influences from languages with which they had been in contact. This meant that the Roma were originally from India, which also accounts for their customs and appearance. Although Rüdiger was not in a position to explain the reasons why the ancestors of the Roma had left India, he hinted that wars and conquests during the early Middle Ages may have driven them out of there and forced them to seek refuge elsewhere.

The British scholar William Marsden spread this information in the United Kingdom. Conclusions similar to those presented by Rüdiger were published shortly afterwards by Heinrich Grellmann, whose book on Gypsies appeared in 1783, and in a later revised edition in 1787. Grellmann included a chapter on language, which became well-known internationally after the appearance of translations of the German original. In contrast to Rüdiger, who was personally acquainted with Gypsies, Grellmann was prejudiced, and his book contributed to the spread of anti-Roma sentiments.

How language can provide historical clues

Language proved an important clue to reconstructing the route which the ancestors of the Roma took when leaving India and migrating to Europe. The German linguist August Pott compiled the first dictionary and grammar of Romani in which different dialects were considered, and this was published in two volumes in 1844-45. Pott identified words appearing in all dialects of Romani that were of Indian, Persian, Armenian, and Greek origin. He concluded that the Roma must have left India and spent some time in Iran, Armenia and the Greek-speaking Byzantine Empire, before reaching central Europe. Since all dialects of Romani shared the same vocabulary items from those languages, the Roma must have migrated to Europe together in one group, and split only after their arrival in Europe. Similar conclusions were later formulated again by the Slovene-Austrian scholar Franz Miklosich, who, like Pott, specialised in the comparative investigation of Romani dialects. Miklosich emphasised the large Greek component in Romani, and suggested that the Roma must have spent a considerable period of time in Greek-speaking territory – which he referred to as "the European homeland of the Gypsies" – before dispersing.

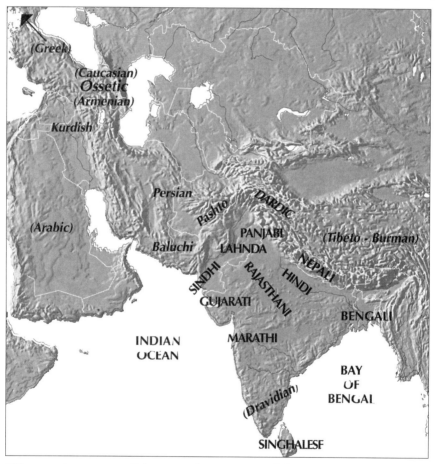

This map shows some of the areas the ancestors of the Roma must have passed through on their journey from India to Europe and the languages spoken in these regions. The route(s) that the Roma took, can perhaps be deduced from the presence of loanwords from Iranian (e.g. Persian and Kurdish), Armenian, Caucasian and Greek in Romani.

Today, linguists are trying to determine the origin of some still obscure vocabulary items in the Romani language. The assumption is that at least some of these are Indian and that others will have been acquired in the Near East or Central Asia, and so they may help identify the routes which Roma took on their way to out of India. But it has also been suggested that the Roma (or rather, their ancestors) might have stayed in one place after their exodus from India. In that area they may have been exposed to various language influences at the same time, or alternatively, some foreign words could have been acquired through contact with travelling traders at markets and fairs, rather than in the regions in which those words were spoken by a native population. It is certainly imaginable that in Medieval Asia Minor (what is now Turkey), Roma would have encountered speakers of Armenian, Greek and Kurdish (an Iranian language, like Persian). They would also have had the opportunity to be near to trade routes from Central Asia (such as the silk route) and interact with travelling merchants.

One of the dilemmas facing linguists when trying to reconstruct the origin of the Romani language is the lack of Arabic words in the vocabulary component that is shared by all Romani dialects. Does this mean that the Roma emigrated to Europe before the Arab conquests of Iran and other parts of Asia in the seventh century? This question lacks a satisfactory answer to this day. But toward the end of the nineteenth century scholars pointed to Arabic sources that mention captives of Indian origin who in the year 837 were brought to Ain Zarba at the border of the Byzantine Empire (in today's Syria), along with their families, and were then taken prisoner by the Greek-speaking Byzantines who raided their camp. The large number of persons involved, some thirteen thousand, suggests that these might have been the core of what was later to become the Near Eastern Dom (who also speak an Indian language) or the Romani nation, but this is by no means certain.

However, it is very difficult to ascertain whether the people referred to in such sources are indeed related to the Roma. Another source that has often been cited in connection with the early history of the Roma is a text by the Persian poet Firdausi, where reference is made to musicians invited from India by the Persian Shah Bahram Gur in the 5th century. The value of such references remains limited, perhaps to the mere recognition that there had always been emmigration of groups from India, whether specialised in certain trades or captives.

17

Other Indic languages outside of India

It is in this connection that one must consider other groups of Indian origin who have, to various degrees, preserved their languages and patterns of social organisation outside of India. These include the Jats of Afghanistan and the Parya of the Central Asian countries Tajikistan and Uzbekistan. There are also groups of Indian origin whose names are similar to those of the Roma. These are the Dom of the Near East (now mainly in Jordan, Lebanon, Palestine, Syria, and Turkey) and the Lom of Armenia. The speech of both these groups was especially studied during the first two decades of the twentieth century, and some connections with Romani were established. The Lom actually speak Armenian, but they use a considerable number of Indic words. From those words it is possible to reconstruct parts of an Indic language which they may have spoken in earlier generations, although the grammatical patterns of this speech remain obscure. The Dom, however, still preserve their language which shows some differences but also many similarities with Romani. Most importantly, all three groups share two important features of identity that may provide some clues as to their background. The first is the name that they use to refer to themselves. It is possible to trace all three names, Rom, Dom and Lom, to just one original Indic root word Dom, since the sound changes from a 'd'-like sound to 'r' and 'l' occur regularly in other words as well. Secondly, the groups share characteristic occupational patterns, for example smiths, musicians and itinerant traders. Scholars following this connection have since assumed an historical origin of all three groups in the Indian Dom, a caste of musicians, metalworkers and others. The Dom of India are not confined to a certain region and their languages vary, although all Indic in origin and structure. There are also groups of Dom such as the Dom of the Hunza valley in northern Pakistan, who left Central India and migrated northwards, but who have preserved their speech and occupational patterns as smiths and musicians.

The association of the Roma with the Dom would help explain both their Indic origin and their social position and economic activities. It would further allow us to place the migration of the Roma out of India in the context of an historically documented, recurring phenomenon of groups of specialised craftsmen and tradesmen who have left the Indian subcontinent over the centuries. This seems attractive especially since recent linguistic investigation has cast serious doubt on the unity of the Rom, Lom and Dom outside of India. It now appears that they left the subcontinent at different times and taking different routes, perhaps accompanying trade caravans. If so, then the similarities in their speech and social-economic features must be more than coincidence.

Some Romani activists and scholars have suggested alternative scenarios in which the Roma were warriors who fought the Muslim invaders and were ultimately pushed as far as Europe in their retreat. There they have since been stigmatised and forced into the social-economic positions that they now occupy. It is not possible to make any firm statements on the basis of what is known now. The Roma could be related to the Indian Ḍom, or descendants of displaced warriors, or neither of these.

Where in India did Romani emerge?

A further mystery is the exact region within India which may have been the original territory occupied by the Roma before their emigration. During the 1920s discussion on this matter flourished among linguists, who attempted to determine this region by finding detailed similarities between Romani and its sister languages in India. When examining the historical development, especially of sounds, in Indian languages, scholars can generally tell whether a language comes from the east, centre or north of India, or whether it dates from the Old, Middle or Modern Indic period. The results for Romani however were contradictory. On the whole, Romani appears to share most features with the so-called Central or Inner languages of India, to which Hindi-Urdu, Punjabi, Gujarati and Rajasthani belong. But in some cases it shares features with Northern Indian languages such as Kashmiri. These shared features of Romani and Northern Indian languages are also found in Old Indian (Sanskrit), but not in modern Indian languages. The British orientalist Ralph Turner concluded from this that the Roma were originally from central India. They would have left this region at a very early stage and moved north, where they remained until their migration away from India.

If, however, we assume an historical connection between the Roma and the Ḍom, then it is possible that there was no coherent territory in which the Roma were settled prior to their emigration, and that their original language had been exposed to various layers of influences from different Indic dialects and idioms as they nomadised. At any rate, the question of the exact origin of Romani within India so far lacks a satisfactory answer. Indeed, if the Roma really do originate in a caste, or several castes, then it is likely that they will have shared the languages of the various populations and regions in which they lived, preserving at the most a particular dialect or accent. It may even be possible that Romani as it is known to us today is the result of various Indic dialects that merged after or during the migration out of India into Europe.

19

II. Nature of the Romani language

This chapter describes the nature of the Romani language. Like all other languages, it has dialects, it has borrowed words from other languages and it has a vocabulary which is sufficient for all needs. There are dictionaries, grammar books, language teaching materials, etc. The chapter also illustrates some of the grammatical rules of the language.

There are many wrong ideas about Romani

We often find, in old fictional works, references to Gypsies and their supposed secrets and mysteries. Their language is often cited in incorrect ways, spreading false ideas about its nature, use and significance. An example is a sixteenth century drama called *La Zingana* ("The Gypsy"), written by the Italian playwright Giancarli. In this play, the character of the Gypsy lady often uses sentences in a kind of Arabic-Italian-Spanish trade language called *Lingua Franca*. Perhaps because the idea that the Gypsies were of Egyptian origin was popular at that time, the author chose to portray this character as speaking a language which was widespread among merchants in the Mediterranean. This language, however, has nothing to do with the language of the Gypsies.

Even now old prejudices and incorrect views are uncritically repeated, thus strengthening a false approach to the matter. Sometimes examples of "Gypsy" words in books are not from Romani at all but from some sort of slang.

VOCABVLA LINGVAE
fictitiæ Zigarorum et mendicorum, ex li-
bello cuius paulò antè men-
tionem fecimus.

K 3

Elemental

Das Elemental vñ Vocabulari
der Rotwelschen Grammatic vnd
spraach / Von den hochgelerten Cāmesierern
in der Wanderschafft beschriben/Das nit ein
yeder Hautz verlunschen vnd Barlen
mög. Ja ein dart vff syn giel.

A

¶Adone	Gott
Achelen	Essen
Alchen	Gon/sich trollen
Alch dich	Gang hyn

mach dich über die wythe/oder
Alch dich übern glentz.

B

¶Breithart	Wythin
Boß	Buß
Boßhart	Fleysch
Boßhartuetzer	Metzger
Betzam	Ein ey
Barlen	Reden

Konrad Gessner, who wrote a book on languages in 1555, was one of the first to confuse Romani with a form of slang – a misunderstanding continuing until now. The Latin heading states that it presents "words of the language of the Gypsies", but it actually gives words from Rotwelsch, a slang or secret language spoken in Germany.

Is Romani a slang or jargon ?

This example leads us immediately to ask a question: is Romani a slang or jargon? A "jargon" is designed as a subcode of a natural language, being a set of words and phrases within a frame of reference which does not differ from the basic language in its standard variety, or a substandard variety. Romani is certainly not a kind of jargon. It is a normal language used for all forms of communication, and learned as a first language by children. It is not just a set of words used only by certain age groups or circles of friends, like slang. Examples are youth slang, Cockney rhyming slang, Latin jargon used by doctors or other in-group vocabulary as used for instance by circus people. Thus, a jargon or slang is characterised mainly by a different vocabulary, a different stock of words. This is clearly not the case for Romani. We will come back to this in Chapter V. Romani is a language in the fullest sense of the term, characterised by a vocabulary of its own and a unique grammatical structure.

Of course, inside the language itself we may observe the use of jargon and slang, but this just proves the status of Romani as a full-fledged language. Romani coppersmiths may use a variety of technical terms not known by others in the community, comparable to a professional jargon such as that of doctors. An example of Romani slang could be the word *bedo* which is used by some Italian Sinti as a cryptic synonym for more common *gadžo* "non-Gypsy" (see Chapter IV). Another example is the use of the word *dešuddu* (*dešuduj*), literally "twelve", used by Roma in Calabria (South Italy) for "judge". This term is used due to the similarity of the Southern Italian pronunciation of the word for judge, *giudice*, which resembles the Italian word for "twelve", *dodici*. An example from England is the word *vonger* "money", which originally meant "coal" and which replaced the old word *lové* in the local Romani.

Is Romani a dialect?

The term "dialect" is used for a form of speech which deviates from some established norm. This norm is often a written form which is used in official publications, newspapers and literature. The distinction between "dialect" and "language" is a political one, and not based on the nature of the language. Some would even say that a language is a dialect with a state and an army behind it. The English standard language is also a dialect, which one could call 'standard dialect'. English, like any other language, has a number of dialects. These dialects differ from the norm or standard language in pronunciation, in words or in structure. However, a dialect is not worth less than a standard language. People may think so because it is different from the generally accepted standard language used in writing and in the media. A decision whether for example Scots is an English dialect, or whether Alsatian, Low German, Swiss German or Luxemburg German (Letzebuergisch) are dialects of German or separate languages has to be made on political and social, not linguistic grounds.

Romani is not a dialect. Romani is a language and like all languages it consists of a number of dialects. In contrast to English, however, and most European languages, there is no generally accepted norm or standard language for Romani, be it spoken nor written. This means that in general all dialects of Romani are equally acceptable for their speakers while all Roma consider their own dialect the "best" or "purest". It should also be said that, even though Romani has its roots in India, Romani is not a dialect of Hindi, Punjabi or Dom or any Indian language, such as the languages of nomads in India, locally called "Gypsies". Romani is a separate language, which differs in important ways from its Indian sister languages.

Some differences between Romani dialects are the result of sound changes that only took place in some regions and not in others. Romani, like all languages, is constantly changing and evolving. Other differences may be due to various influences from other languages. This is more clearly the case in Romani than in most western standard languages: Roma are multilinguals, and influences from the other languages they speak can affect their Romani, whereas this is less likely in large monolingual speech communities. Also the fact that Romani has no generally used standard language contributed to the development of dialect differences.

The vocabulary of Romani may not appear to be uniform. This is due to the existence of a variety of dialects, or geographical varieties deriving from the long diaspora of the people. The bulk of the vocabulary, however, is always the same. The existence of dialects of the language, on the other hand, is a further proof that Romani is a real and vital language.

Where do Romani words come from?

The basic vocabulary of Romani in all its variants has an Indian basis. Thus, parts of the body, natural features, family members, common objects, verbs relating to basic needs and actions, common adjectives, numbers, etc. are almost all of Indian origin. Some 700 Indian roots have been identified which are in general use. It is widely accepted by linguists that this culture-free vocabulary (that is to say, words not related to any particular culture) is the most stable in any language. We may therefore safely assume that the Indian vocabulary is the most ancient layer of the language, the part which forms its main identity.

As mentioned above, there are also different layers of non-Indic words, mostly from Asian languages, which are common to all varieties of Romani. In the preceding chapter we have mentioned borrowings from Iranian languages (perhaps seventy), Armenian (around fourty), Greek (a few hundred) and a few words from Georgian. These are found in all Romani dialects. Apart from these, which are common to all forms of Romani, there are dialects with borrowings from German, Hungarian, Romanian, Turkish and Slavic languages – plus words from countries where the speakers currently reside. Which languages these are depends on where the speakers of this dialect are living or where they have lived before. These European words in Romani differ from dialect to dialect. Romani is comparable with English, which also has borrowed words from many languages.

Romani is not corrupted by borrowings

All languages can take over words or even structures from other languages. This is an entirely normal process. Usually a vernacular, or a spoken language, takes over words from a more dominant or official language. It also happens that words are taken over from a foreign language because a new item has been imported from that area. English took over words like *curry* or *bungalow* from Indian languages because these were things for which English did not have a word. But if there is strong pressure from an official language, even common words can sometimes be borrowed. English, for instance, borrowed many words from French when French was the official language of England in the late Middle Ages. Therefore English has the French borrowing *liberty* beside earlier *freedom*, and *ancient* beside earlier *old*. In fact, almost half of the common words in English are of French origin. Additionally there are words from more than a dozen other languages (African, American Indian, etc.) in English. It is sometimes said that English is such a rich language because it has such a large vocabulary and so many words in the dictionary. Nevertheless, no one would say that English is a "poor language" or a "corrupted language" for that reason. If one were to count the words in a dictionary of English, however, only a small percentage would be original English or Anglo-Saxon (Old English) words. It is therefore very difficult for present-day speakers of English to read and understand Old English.

In short, Romani, like other languages, has taken over words from other languages. Some people have claimed that this makes Romani a corrupted language. This is clearly a biased view: the same process which has "enriched" English has supposedly "corrupted" Romani.

In the case of Romani, however, the situation is more complicated since Roma live in so many different countries and have taken over words from a variety of other languages differing from region to region. Since borrowings for words like "refrigerator" or "glasses" are from different languages in the different varieties of Romani, these words differ from one dialect to another.

The grammatical system of Romani is not so much affected by borrowing. In general, grammatical elements are much less often borrowed than words. If we look at the Romani case endings of the nouns or the verb endings, it is easy to see that these are very similar to those of Indian languages. This Indian origin of the grammatical system is confirmed by the presence of other Indian grammatical traits.

Table 1: Some endings in Romani

	Romani	*Sanskrit*	*Hindi and/or Punjabi*
plural masculine	-e	-	-e
plural feminine	-a	-āḥ	-
object masculine singular	-es	-a-sya	-e
dative 'to'	-ke	(kakṣā)	ko
instrumental 'with'	-sa	samam	se
ablative 'from'	-tar	tarite	te

What can we learn from loanwords?

One of the reasons that people borrow words is because they describe things that are new to them. Romani words relating to travel, for instance, sometimes appear to be from Iranian languages or from Armenian, perhaps because those languages were spoken in the countries their ancestors passed through when they left India. So we find *vurdón* "carriage, wagon", now also often used to mean "automobile", from Iranian (perhaps Ossetic), and *grast* or *grai* "horse", from Armenian. The presence of Iranian words for things such as "sea" (*dor-jav*) and "church" (*khangerí*, originally "turret") also suggests that the migrants encountered particular features, buildings, flowers, trees, etc. for the first time after they had left India.

In the same way most terms relating to metallurgy appear to be Greek. Romani has a considerable core of Greek borrowings, perhaps as many as a few hundred words. This may be the result of a long period of residence in Greek-speaking areas, where new techniques were learnt or old ones revamped. Some examples can be found in Table 2.

Table 2: Some Romani metallurgical terms borrowed from Greek

Romani	Greek	English
(v)amoni	amoni	anvil
kakavi	kakkavi	kettle
molivi	molyvi, molivdos	lead
petalo	petalo(n)	horseshoe
karfin	karfi	nail
(i)sviri	sfiri	hammer

There are also a few grammatical endings in Romani which are borrowed from Greek. Grammatical endings are elements such as in English: *-ed*, *-s*, *-hood*, *-ity*, *-al*, *-ly*, etc. For instance, some Romani varieties use the ending *-mos* (originally from Greek) to form abstract nouns, whereas most others use Indian *-ipe(n)*. The word for "truth" in different dialects illustrates this: some say *čačipe* and others *čačimos*. Another example of a borrowed ending is the element *-to*. This makes cardinal numerals into so-called ordinal (rank) numbers, e.g. *duj* "two", *dujto* "second", *štar* "four", *štarto* "second". This ending, also borrowed from Greek, is present in all Romani dialects. Borrowing of such elements is not so common in languages, but it does happen under pressure from a dominant language. From this we can conclude that Greek once was an important language in the society of the ancestors of the Roma, and again that there must have been long and intensive contact between Greek and Romani.

How many words are there in the Romani language?

The number of words in Romani is also a pertinent question which deserves a reply capable of contradicting some common misunderstandings. As mentioned earlier, it is sometimes said that Romani has a "poor" or a "limited" vocabulary, and in many cases short word-lists tend to confirm this idea. Many published vocabularies of Romani do not list modern borrowings from neighbouring languages. This is a flaw due to the belief that the words of the language must be "original". Often only "pure" language is sought out for descriptive publications. This is especially the case with older publications. In fact these word lists often avoid borrowings either because they are not considered part of the (original) language, or because they are not of immediate interest to the linguist in question. These lists may also reflect the lack of knowledge in the researcher of the richness of the vocabulary he or she has investigated.

As a matter of fact, the Romani vocabulary has developed according to the needs of the different communities of speakers. Every living language reacts according to the situations in which it is used. New words are created or borrowed when this is useful and necessary. Romani is well suited for the communities which use it, and the language changes if the situation requires it to do so.

Several studies have shown that people understand passively some 10,000 to 20,000 words in their language. Nevertheless, dictionaries of these languages may contain more than 100,000 words. Many of these are specialist terms. It appears, however, that people use some 2,000 to 6,000 words actively in their daily lives. This is true for most European languages, and probably for Romani speakers as well. When counting the number of words in a language, it therefore makes a huge difference whether one counts the words used on a daily basis or all the words listed in a complete dictionary which includes dialect words, professional terms, specialised vocabulary and old-fashioned words.

For all these reasons, it is not easy to estimate the number of words existing in Romani. The most thorough dictionary is that of Norbert Boretzky and Birgit Igla, which was published in 1994. This contains some 10,000 words used in Romani in south-eastern Europe. This number is comparable with figures for other European languages. The core vocabulary of Romani, that is, those words which are not borrowed from European languages, is the same in all dialects, with only some minor differences. This core vocabulary contains approximately 1,000 words. Most of these have been identified as being from Indian and Iranian languages, Armenian and Byzantine Greek and even a few from Georgian, a language of the South Caucasus. There are still some 100 words whose roots have not been traced. This is about the same as the number of Anglo-Saxon stems in English, another language with a great number of borrowings. In short, Romani does not differ from other languages as to the number of words.

Are there dictionaries of Romani?

There are a few dozen published dictionaries of Romani. Not all of these are good or reliable. Some cover only one dialect or one regional variety, others are compilations with words from several dialects, sometimes relying on previous sources. A list of some useful Romani-English dictionaries is given on page 128. Volume 2 will provide a more complete list, including dictionaries of Romani to languages other than English.

Is the language always called Romani?

Speakers of Romani usually call the language "Romanes" or "Romani čhib", not just "Romani", as is the custom in publications. Romani is an abbreviated form of *Romani čhib*, "the Romani tongue". The word "Romani" is an adjective derived from the noun "Rom", and it roughly means "relating to Gypsies". The noun "rom" means "husband" in all dialects and in most forms of Romani also "Gypsy". The word "Romanes" is an adverb and means "like a Rom". The word 'Romani' (sometimes spelled "Romany" in English) is most often used in the literature about the language, although most speakers say "Romanes".

Even though not all speakers of Romani would call themselves "Roma", virtually all call their language "Romanes". Groups who call themselves "Kalo" (Finland, Wales), "Sinti" (Germany and elsewhere), "Manouche" (Southern France) or "Romanichal" (England) call their language "Romanes", or used to do so in earlier documented periods. Despite the different names for their own group, they speak the same language and give it the same name.

Slightly different ways of referring to the language may exist. There are also labels such as *amari čhib* "our language". The Havati and Sloveni Roma in Italy would say *vrakeri po románe* "speaking in the Rom way", and in the Burgenland the name *Roman* is used.

So far, we have discussed only the names that Romanies themselves use for their language. Outsiders also have a variety of labels for the language, derived from their name for the Romani people, for instance Cyganskij, Çingene, Tsigane, Zigeunerisch, Zingarico, etc. Most Romanies dislike these terms, as they are often negative and derogatory. The name Romani or Romanes is to be preferred.

Is Romani a secret language?

It is a commonly held belief that the language of the Sinti and Roma is a secret language. In general this is not true. It is a normal language without any restrictions on use and spoken without a special aim of secrecy. Furthermore, there are dictionaries, grammar books and magazines in Romani and anyone can buy them and learn the language.

There are groups, however, who consider their language as belonging to their group only, and they do not want to disclose anything of it to outsiders. They see Romani as the language of the Roma. But other Roma will be proud when outsiders take an interest in their language. Both at a group level and at the individual level there is a wide range of different attitudes of the Roma towards their language.

The various Roma groups have different attitudes towards an outsider ("Gadžo") who want to learn Romani. Some settled Servika Roma in Slovakia feel flattered if a Gadžo speaks to them in Romani. In nearly every Slovak village there are some Gadžos who have learned Romani. The Sinti in Western Europe and the Kalé in Finland, however, prefer to keep their language secret and do not disclose it to outsiders. In Germany, the Sinti remember that during the Nazi period racial scientists learnt the language in order to get close to the community and build up family trees which were later used to seek out Sinti and send them to concentration camps. The reason why Finnish (and English) Gypsies are wary of outsiders learning their language is because they see it – or remember it in the past – as a valuable tool for secret communication in situations of conflict with the authorities over, for example, camping sites.

This difference in attitude also affects the written literature: whereas Slovak Roma write in Romanes, the Sinti author Philomena Franz writes only in German even though she speaks Romani fluently.

Some Roma parents tell their children not to disclose anything about the language to outsiders. It is therefore possible that Romani children will not want to say anything in their own language in class, in contrast to children from other ethnic groups, since they were told not to share their language with others. Not all Romani groups and individuals do so, however.

Does Romani have a grammar?

The word "grammar" has two meanings. First, it means a system of rules used by speakers of a language, as discussed before. It also has a second meaning: a written description of a language. It is not the goal of this book to say much about the grammatical structure of Romani, or to enable readers to learn the language. Nevertheless, we would like to give some impression of its structure, in order to show that it is a real language, in some sense comparable with respected languages such as German, Greek, Latin and Sanskrit.

Linguists distinguish different classes of words. The most important of these are *verbs* (actions or situations, e.g. "to sleep", "to crawl", "to hit"), *substantives* or *nouns* (objects or ideas, e.g. "man", "house", "love", "linguistics"), *adjectives* (e.g. "black", "big", "loud"), *prepositions* (e.g. "in", "at", "about", etc.), *articles* ("the", "a"). Further we can mention *adverbs*, which say something about the manner, time or place of an action or situation verb (e.g. "loudly", "here" or "tomorrow") and pronouns ("I", "me", "him", etc). Romani also has these word classes, and more, but we don't discuss them all. As an illustration, we list on the next page some common proposals for such linguistic terms in Romani.

New words formed for grammatical terms

The first description of Romani grammar written in Romani was made by by a Rom teacher Šaip Yusuf from Skopje, Macedonia. With the linguist Krume Kepeski he published a 220-page bilingual (Romani-Macedonian) textbook Romani gramatika – Romska gramatika *in Skopje 1980. Fourteen years later a 238-page textbook of Romani with a grammatical description written in Romani was published in Rumania: Gheorghe Sarău,* Limba romani, Bucharest 1994. *Although Roma have always discussed their language, its vocabulary, its "purity", comparison with other Romani dialects and the future of Romani, the discussions were not carried out at a theoretical linguistic level. That is why common linguistic terms are missing – and the authors of the two grammars mentioned had to find them, or rather "create" them. It seems that Gheorghe Sarau, who wrote his book later, was not influenced by the Macedonian authors, as his terminology differs. Also in the Czech Republic attempts have been made to coin at least the main linguistic terms in Romani. Dr Vlado Oláh, the president of the Roma cultural organisation Matice Romska, organised a one week workshop in September 1995 dedicated to Romani. It was attended by twenty-five Roma journalists, writers, and actors from the theatre Romathan (Košice, Slovak Republic). The participants of the seminar after collective discussions presented suggestions for some grammatical terms in Romani. For the reader's interest we will give a comparison of selected linguistic terminology in Romani coined by the participants of the workshop, by Šaip Yusuf and by Gheorghe Sarau. These neologisms were created independently of each other. They can be found on the next page.*

	workshop	Šaip Yusuf	Gheorghe Sarău
substantives	bare/šerutne nava	anavjora	navne
adjectives	kijathode nava	dodine	pašnavne
pronouns	vašonava	isthanardine	sarnavne
numerals	ginde	gjende	ginavne
verbs	kerutne	keripne	keravne
adverbs	paškerutne	sakaje	paškernavne
prepositions	anglonava	bachanne	-
conjunctions	phandune	phandavne	konžunkciji
interjections	akharde lava	interjekcije	-
particles	lavora	lafjori	-
article	artiklos	dženo	artiklos

We can see that the specific Romani system of word formation yields enough devices to form new terms for new things. It is also interesting to observe that in quite a number of cases the new terms in the three colums are derived in a similar way, although the derivational suffixes and/or the phonetic form of the word may differ according to the dialect.

Linguists also look at how these words *function* in a sentence. In English, for instance, you know that normally the first noun in a sentence is the one which does an action: "the boy sleeps" or "the man bit the dog", and the second noun is the one which undergoes the action. The first is called *subject*, the other *object*. In English, you also get a form change with a few words, depending on whether they are subject (actor) or object (undergoer). Compare "I see him" with "He sees me", where "I" and "me" refer to the same person, and also "he" and "him". By the way, in this sentence also the form of the verb changes, depending on who is the actor, "I" or "he/she".

Languages can express the function of the words in many different ways. English makes mostly use of word order, and also to some extent a change in the form of words (he/him, they/them, see/sees, bold/boldly, man/men). Other languages add something to words to show what is an object and what is a subject, so-called "case endings" as in e.g. German or Latin.

Romani nouns

The Romani noun changes its endings to show differences in meaning, i.e. it has case endings. These endings also show the function of that word in a sentence. Here is one example:

sap	snake, subject of a sentence (a snake is on the branch)
sapes	snake, object of a sentence (I saw a snake)
sapeske	"to a snake"
sapestar	"from a snake"
sapesa	"with a snake"
sapeste	used after a preposition, e.g. *tela sapeste* "under a snake"
sapesko	"of a snake", for example a snake's bite.

In other words, Romani has a system of case endings similar to Latin. It has nominatives, genitives, datives, accusatives, vocatives and ablatives like Latin and Greek. But Romani has two more case endings: an instrumental ("with") and a locative ("in, at"). The classical languages of Europe and India all had case endings, but in many modern languages such as English, French and Italian, these have disappeared. Romani has preserved the case system, even though several dialects tend to replace some of the cases with prepositions (e.g. "in", "above", "with"). This parallels changes in some of the European languages. For example Greek has lost three out of six cases.

The Romani case system functions somewhat differently from the Latin system. In Latin there are five different sets of all the case endings. These five so-called "declensions" show different endings in each set. The endings for "one snake" (singular) and for "two/many snakes" (plural) show different forms in Latin. In Romani there is only one set of case endings for singular and plural. The other difference is that the Romani case endings are added to a special form of the word, which is also used for ordinary grammatical objects. The word *Rom*, for instance, is *Romes* in the accusative, and if you want to say "from the Gypsy man" you say *Romestar*. The ending *-tar* (and the other endings as well) is added to the form *Romes*, and not to *Rom*.

Romani verbs

Romani verbs have different endings, depending on who is performing the action (e.g. "I", "you", "he", "she", "we", "they"). The one who performs the action is called the *subject*. Romani verbs are comparable with those in languages like Italian, Latin or Spanish. In such languages the personal pronoun

("I", 'he", "she", etc.) is not used, because the verb already indicates who is the subject.

Table 3: Present tense verbs in Romani, Spanish, Latin and Italian

English	Romani	Spanish	Latin	Italian
I love, want	kam-av	quier-o	am-o	am-o
You love	kam-es	quier-es	am-as	am-i
He/she loves	kam-el	quier-e	am-at	am-a
We love	kam-as	quer-emos	am-amus	am-iamo
You love	kam-en	quier-en	am-atis	am-ate
They love	kam-en	quier-en	am-ant	am-ano

There is no original infinitive form ("to do", "to walk", etc.) in Romani. Romani verb endings always indicate the subject of the sentence. If you want to say "I want to go" in Romani, you have to say "I want that I go" (*kamav te džav*). Some Romani dialects do have infinitives, but it is clear that these are newer developments. By the way, not all existing languages have infinitive forms. In Europe, for instance, the languages of the Balkans also lack infinitives.

Romani also has a number of other verb endings which can change the meaning of a word. The verb *dikhel* means "she/he sees", but the derived verb *dikhjol* means roughly "it is visible", hence also "it seems, it is obvious".

The past tense in Romani is usually formed with an element such as *d*, *l*, *n*, and *t* between the stem and the ending. The subject-denoting endings used in the past tense are completely different from the endings used in the present tense in Romani. This can be seen in Table 4.

Table 4: Present and past verbal endings in Romani

	present tense	past tense
I listen(ed)	šun-av "I listen"	šun-d-um, šun-d-om, šun-d-em
"I listened"		
you listen(ed)	šun-es	šun-d-an, šun-d-al
he/she listen(ed)	šun-el	šun-d-as/šun-d-a
we listen(ed)	šun-as	šun-d-am
you listen(ed)	šun-en	šun-d-an
they listen(ed)	šun-en	šun-d-e

It is also possible to add an ending *-as* (some dialects *-ahi*) to these verbs, which gives it a so-called "imperfective meaning", i.e. the action may take some time, or may still continue. Thus *šun-av-as* would mean "I was listening" and *šun-d-om-as* "I had been listening".

Romani does not have a verb "to have". This is also the case in languages like Finnish, Irish, Russian, Welsh and many others. These languages use the verb "to be" to express possession, roughly "It is with/to me". This absence is merely a grammatical device, and it has nothing to do with dispossession or nomadism, and it is not a sign of a deficient language.

Romani gender, articles and adjectives

Romani has two grammatical genders, like many European and Asian languages. These are labelled "masculine" and "feminine". The first are used for men and the second for women. Other nouns also belong to either of these groups, and the genders are chosen more or less arbitrarily.

Like most European languages, Romani has so-called "definite articles", translatable in English by "the". Many languages do not have such articles.

The forms of the articles, almost all adjectives and some verbs show different endings depending on the gender of the noun: *baro manuš* "big/important man" versus *bari rani* "big/important lady". Romani has different articles for masculine and feminine nouns, for subject and non-subject and for singular and plural articles. In this respect it is roughly comparable with German, which also has a number of different articles depending on gender, number (singular, plural) or case of the noun to which it refers (*die*, *das*, *dem*, *den*, *der*, etc.).

Romani also distinguishes between beings that are alive ("animate") and things that are not alive ("inanimate"). These two types of nouns have different forms when they are the object of an action ("I see the *snake*" versus "I see the *house*").

Animate nouns get an accusative ending and inanimate nouns do not, and they have different definite articles. If one says "I see the dog" one would say *me dikhava e džukles*, but for "I see the house" one would say *me dikhava o kher*. The word *džukel* "dog" has an ending *-es*, but the word *kher* "house" does not.

35

Romani word order

Word order in Romani sentences is flexible. In a normal story the most common word order is: first the verb, then the subject (e.g.: "bites the dog"). This is very different from English, where the order is: first the subject, then the verb (e.g. "the dog bites"). If there are both a subject and an object, the most common order in Romani would be: verb – object – subject ("bites the stick the dog"), but if something unexpected happens, the order is rather subject – verb – object ("the man sees the dog"). In Romani, many different word orders are allowed, in contrast to a language like English.

Romani sound system

The sound system of Romani does not differ dramatically from European languages in most respects. Nevertheless, a number of rare sounds, such as so-called "aspirated stops", are present in virtually all dialects of Romani. Apart from the sounds 'k', 't' and 'p', Romani has these same sounds with an h-like sound immediately behind it. In Romani this is written with an 'h' after that letter. For example the word *kandel* means "she/he listens", but *khandel* means "she/he/it stinks". This sound distinction is rarely found in European languages.

Of course not all features of this language are unique. Romani shares many grammatical traits with other languages. But the whole of it forms a unique corpus of rules which in its totality make the Romani language a unique form of speech.

Is there a grammar book of the Romani language?

The grammar of a language can be described in a grammar book. There are dozens of published grammars or grammatical descriptions of Romani. Some of these try to portray a form of general Romani, emphasising all the common traits, whereas others just describe one specific dialect. There is even a printed grammar of Romani which is based on the language as spoken by just one man. The titles of some good grammatical descriptions in English are given on page 129. These can be found in libraries or in some cases ordered in bookstores.

From the preceding description it is clear that Romani has its own grammatical system. This grammatical system is shared by all varieties, from Wales to Finland and from Southern Italy to Siberia and Iran. In all these areas there are people who speak a European form of Romani. There may be some grammatical differences from one dialect to another, as in all languages.

This suffices to give a rough impression of the language. We hope we have made clear that Romani is not some jargon or an incomplete language. It is a language like English, German, Hindi, Italian, Latin or Russian, but still clearly different from all of them. Romani structure and vocabulary are fully developed and capable of expressing all the needs of the community of its speakers.

More than a dozen grammars of Romani and its dialects have been published.

III. Language use

In this chapter we will discuss who speaks Romani, when, why, where and how. We will discuss some rules of language use which differ from non-Romani etiquette and which may lead to misunderstandings and unintended insults. Connected to this is the question of how Romani is learned. It will start with the difficult estimate of how many people actually speak Romani.

How many people speak Romani?

It is always difficult to estimate the number of speakers of a language. This is even more so with a language like Romani. The total number of speakers of Romani is unknown. There are several reasons for this. First, many Roma hide their identity to avoid being discriminated against, and they may also deny speaking the language. Many Roma still remember times when being a Rom was in itself equivalent to a death sentence, most recently during the Second World War and in the Yugoslav War. Secondly, in most countries Romani is not a recognised language. Even if the national census covers language-related questions, the questions or possible answers may not include Romani. Neither is it possible to derive the number of speakers of Romani in a given country from the number of Roma living there – insofar that is known. In Finland and Hungary many Roma no longer speak Romani. Finally, the total number of Roma around the world is also difficult to estimate. It may be between ten and twenty million. The European countries which have the largest populations are Bulgaria, Romania, Slovakia, Spain and Russia. It is estimated that there

Table 5: The approximate number of Romani speakers in Europe		
Country	**Approximate number of Romani speakers**	**Approximate percentage of Gypsy population that speaks Romani**
Albania	90,000	95 %
Austria	18,000	80 %
Belarus	27,000	94 %
Belgium	10,000	80 %
Bosnia-Hercegovina	40,000	90 %
Bulgaria	600,000	80 %
Croatia	28,000	80 %
Cyprus	650	90 %
Czech Republic	140,000	50 %
Denmark	1,500	90 %
Estonia	1,150	90 %
Finland	3,000	40 %
France	215,000	70 %
Germany	85,000	70 %
Greece	160,000	90 %
Hungary	290,000	50 %
Italy	80,000	80 %
Kazakhstan	42,000	90 %
Latvia	18,700	90 %
Lithuania	4,100	90 %
Luxembourg	100	80 %
Macedonia	215,000	90 %
Moldova	56,000	90 %
Netherlands	7,000	90 %
Norway	200	90 %
Poland	56,000	90 %
Portugal	50	- %
Romania	1,030,000	90 %
Russia	405,000	80 %
Serbia-Montenegro	380,000	90 %
Slovakia	300,000	60 %
Slovenia	8,000	90 %
Spain	1,000	1 %
Sweden	9,500	90 %
Turkey	280,000	70 %
Ukraine	113,000	90 %
United Kingdom	1,000	0.5 %

may be some eight to twelve million speakers of Romani in the world today (including the Americas and Australia).

The table on p. 40 lists the estimated number of Romani speakers in most European countries and tells us what percentage this is of the Gypsy population. If we add the figures we get almost five million speaking the language from a total of approximately five million Roma. This is the most precise estimate we can give for Europe. There are also Romani speakers in almost all South American and Central American countries as well as in Australia, South Africa, the United States and the former Soviet Asian republics. It should be noted that this table counts only the number of speakers of Romani proper, as described in the previous chapter, not Para-Romani. Para-Romani is a overall term for languages where Romanies have combined the vocabulary of Romani with the structure of another language in ingenious ways. If we were to add those, we would perhaps get between 50,000 and 300,000 extra speakers mainly from Portugal, Scandinavia, Spain and the United Kingdom. These varieties will be discussed in more detail below in Chapter V.

Are there Romani speakers who speak no other language?

Virtually all speakers of Romani are at least bilingual, that is to say, they speak at least one other language in addition to Romani. Romani children generally learn Romani as their first language, but they may also acquire another language at the same time, or they will when they start school. In most Romani homes languages other than Romani are also heard, not least because there is a radio or a television. In such cases Romani children will grow up with two or even more languages.

Children can absorb many languages easily. Many children in the world learn more than one language before school age. Only in most of western Europe and America is it common to learn only one (with exceptions such as Catalonia, Wales, etc.). Bilingualism is not detrimental to the child's development. Many studies have in fact shown that knowing more than one language helps to develop the child's psychological and analytical skills.

The only monolingual Roma (that is, Roma who speak no language other than Romani) are children of pre-school age. The number of adult monolingual Romani speakers is negligible. Roma speak the official language of the country where they live. They need to know these languages in order to communicate with non-Romani administrators, colleagues, customers, friends, neighbours, shopkeepers and teachers.

Are there Roma who have lost
their language or who do not speak Romani?

In many countries there are Roma who do not want to be identified as Roma. They may refuse to speak their mother tongue in public or even in the home. Their children grow up without any knowledge of Romani. They use the dominant language of the country. For example the community of Muslim Roma in Bulgaria do not use Romani in their everyday communication, but Turkish. Their children speak only Turkish. Many Christian Roma in Bulgaria prefer to speak Bulgarian and their children learn only Bulgarian, without any knowledge of Romani. This phenomenon can be observed in other countries as well, for example in the Czech Republic, Finland, Hungary, Romania, Slovakia, Spain and Turkey.

In a number of cases formerly bilingual groups of Roma have shifted away recently from Romani to their other language, e.g. to Turkish in Bulgaria and Turkey, and to Romanian in Romania.

When is Romani spoken and to whom?

Romani is mainly spoken in the home, with Romani neighbours and during encounters with other Romanies. Generally speaking, it is a language spoken only by Roma, and especially within their own communities. Of course, occasionally a non-Romani person is adopted into a Romani family or marries a Romani man or woman, and he or she would naturally learn Romani as well. Outside their own community, Roma speak the dominant language of the region or the official language of the country.

Where do Roma learn their language?

All children in all societies learn to speak their language or languages from their parents and playmates. This is also the case for Romani children. Unfortunately, until about 1990, the language development of Romani children was not investigated. Not many scholars were interested in studying this topic. Since then, there have been a few studies of the early learning of Romani by very small children, between the ages one and three. These recent studies show what all Roma knew, namely that Romani is learned in the family, especially through interaction between the mother and the child. Here is an example of a dialogue between a Romani mother and her child of one year and one month, where the mother stimulates her child to imitate her speech:

Mother:	Saly, phen-ta da-da [*Saly, say da-da*]
Child:	da-da
Mother:	Choko [Choko is a name]
Child:	Choko
Mother:	te-te
Child:	te-te

The way that the parents introduce new words to their children (naming the object, repeating and correcting the errors of the children), is the same among Roma as in other families.

In other words, Romani children acquire Romani in the same way as other children learn their languages, and studies show that they follow the universal path of child development in the area of early language acquisition. Some parts of the grammar of languages are apparently easier to learn for children than other parts, and those are roughly the same for all children, irrespective of the language they are learning.

The following interaction shows that very young children repeat exactly the same sounds as the mother. The mother jokingly asks her daughter whether she wants lipstick on her lips. The child (now one year and two months old) answers her mother:

Mother:	Saly, tu ko restoranti ka zhas li? Si li tut lolipe?
	[*Saly, are you going to the restaurant? Do you have lipstick?*]
Child:	a-a-a
Mother:	Ayde te makas tut lolipe! Kate ka makas tut lolipe, kate?
	[*Come to put on your lipstick. Where will I put the lipstick on you, where?*
Child:	va-va

These conversations show that the topics used by Roma parents with their young children are the same as those used by other parents. Children learn to speak through conversation with adults. Even though they are not able to put together long sentences or express abstract ideas at an early age, children do understand the meaning before they can express it. The early language socialisation of Romani children is the same as that which occurs in child development generally, even though there are culture-specific characteristics which influence the shape and the content of the exchanges.

Romani is not learned on the road

In contrast to what many outsiders think, the vast majority of the Roma in the world live in houses, and not in tents or caravans. Only some Roma are nomadic, and among those there are many who live in houses most of the year and who travel during a few months in the summer. This happens mostly in France, Scotland and former Yugoslavia.

Some Roma engage in "commercial nomadism". This means that they make a living by trading or providing services in different places, to which they travel. Here too, Romani is acquired in the family, which may at times or in particular seasons change its place of residence. The language is learned from the mothers. Some groups of commercial nomads have developed their own dialects of Romani.

Politeness among Roma

Politeness is a universal cultural value. All societies recognise situations in which one must "be on one's best behaviour" and in which people are entitled to special respect. One of the ways to show this is to speak respectfully, and to do this the speaker must know what the "rules" are. Rules of politeness vary from culture to culture. This includes rules on speaking politely. A speaker learns not only the structural or grammatical rules of a language, but he or she will also master the whole verbal and non-verbal code of appropriate speech. Knowing these rules diminishes the risk of misunderstanding or conflicts in communication.

Most of the Romani used in this section on politeness refers to the Servika Roma in the Czech and Slovak Republics. However, the same patterns are observable in other Romani groups as well, only the wording may be somewhat different.

The term for "politeness" in many dialects of Romani is *pačiv* or *pativ*. It also means "respect, honour, cultural behaviour". The phrase *te del pativ*, literally "to give respect", also means "to provide food, to show hospitality". People who know how to be polite have always been very much appreciated. It is said: *pačiv des, pačiv xudes* "if you are polite (can show respect), you will be treated politely". An illustration can be given from this traditional song text:

Romani children learn the Romani language from their mothers.

Ko si lašo gavaleri
nek torď arel i mesali
torď arla la de muro dad
mer vov lašo gavaleri

He who is a good gentleman
will make a feast
My father will make a feast
because he is a good gentleman

The Vlax Roma in the Czech Republic sometimes call themselves *mesajake Roma* or *mesaljake Roma*, literally "Roma of the table", from *mesali* "table", by which they mean that they are polite, cultured Roma. These terms show that hospitality is considered one of the highest values in traditional Romani communities. Food is offered to anybody who comes for a visit, without asking the guests whether they are hungry or not. It is in fact very impolite to ask guests: "Are you hungry?" The guest should eat, or taste at least a little to show that he or she does not dislike (*na džungl'ol*) the food and the family where it is served. The hostess usually adds a sentence *Amen sam žuže Roma* "we are clean Roma", with which she means that they do not eat certain kinds of food which are considered ritually unclean, such as horse-meat, dog-meat, donkey or pork.

Furthermore, it is impolite amongst these Roma to thank the host for providing food. If a guest does so, the hosts may reply *Ma pal'iker, ma pal'iker, na sal ko Gadže* "Don't thank (us), don't thank (us), you are not among non-Roma". It is the hosts who should thank the guest for this opportunity to demonstrate their hospitality.

Asking and thanking

In many non-Romani societies, the polite way to ask for something is to start with a phrase such as "please ....", "be so kind...", "could you possibly..." and so on. These are not always used in Romani society. Roma in the Czech Republic simply say "Give me ....", for example *De man cigaretl'a* "Give me a cigarette", *de man te pijel/de man pañi* "give me something to drink/give me water", *xude mange mri taška*, "pass me my bag". Services like these are seen as natural rather than as a form of kindness, and they are not usually thanked for. In Romani communities, therefore, not thanking for this is not considered impolite. Roma often continue to follow this rule when they speak other languages. This may sound rude to others, but in fact they are simply transferring the patterns from their first language.

If the service or object being asked for is felt to be less "natural" or somewhat troublesome, the request may be expressed more politely: first of all by using the right tone of voice and facial expression, secondly by slight changes of phrasing. For example, the word *ča* "only", may be added to the request: *De man ča cigaretl'a* "give me a cigarette". One can also use a special ending called a diminutive which is normally used for little things: *phen ča mange paramisori* "tell me 'only' a 'little' tale". In either case, the effect is to present the request as an insignificant one.

Oaths

Roma use many oaths. Some oaths are standard expressions, others are improvised on the spot. They are used to stress the truth of something said, or to downplay something said by others. Some examples are: *te merav dži tosara* "may I be dead by the morning!" This emphasises the truth of a preceding statement of the speaker. An expression like *te na vakeres ča te bašos* "may you not speak but only bark!" said by a mother-in-law to her daughter-in-law if she speaks back, is a reaction of the hearer to inappropriate behaviour. Oaths are extremely rich in form and content.

Taboo words

Roma avoid the use of certain words in public. Again, Roma do not differ from others. However, the range of taboo words or subjects may differ. Sometimes topics and issues which are taboo in one community may not be taboo in another one. There are some general subjects, such as parts of the human body, which cannot be discussed between a man and a woman. Sexually related topics are not possible in conversation between young and old generations. Deceased persons are not discussed either, as is everything related to the lavatory. Finally, names for diseases are not usually mentioned. Some of these taboos are the same as in the surrounding communities. Here again, it may lead to misunderstanding and irritation in both directions when the range of taboos differ.

Greetings

When people meet, they greet each other, and how they do this depends partly on who they are: men or women, older or younger, friends or strangers. When two people who know each other meet outside, they ask *Kaj džas? Kaj*

47

salas/sanas? "Where are you going? Where have you been?" When Polish Roma meet each other, they ask *Syr tuke kerel?* "How are you doing?" It is expected that the answer will be true. Such a greeting and its answer are a form of the social control which is so important in the traditional Romani community. Every individual is watched by everybody else, or as the Roma would say: *tel e jakh* "under the eye".

The question *sar sal/ sar san* "how are you?" is answered with *mišto/lačho* "well!" or *the avka the avka.* "so so". The greeting *lačho dives* "good day" is also used. It may be embellished with *te del o Del lačho dives* "may God give (you) a good day". When someone is leaving, the one who stays says: *dža Devlesa/dža Devleha* literally "go with God", or: *džan Devlesa/džan Devleha* to more than one person. The one who is leaving says *Ačh(en) Devlesa/ Ačh(en) Devleha* "Stay with God". When someone sets out on a longer journey, one says *baxtalo drom*, literally "happy road".

Romani folklore

The folklore of the Roma is very rich and it has many important socio-cultural functions in traditional Romani communities. The two most formalised genres are *paramisa/parmiča/pamarisla* (tales) and *gil'a/d'ija* (songs).

Traditional tales

Paramisa in many Romani communities are told on various occasions. The most formal one is a gathering – often attended by even more than hundred Roma – at which strict cultural norms have to be observed. At such gatherings the *paramisaris* (narrator) is nearly always a man. People meet in the biggest house in the Roma colony. Sometimes some money is collected to pay the owner of the house. In winter each listener will bring a log of wood to keep up the fire. The *paramisaris* is rewarded with tobacco, sometimes also with money, especially if he is invited for story telling from some distant village. During his performance nobody is supposed to interrupt or to talk. That is why little children are often not admitted to such gatherings. On the other hand, the public is supposed to react with sighs of awe or laughter which is a way of appreciation for the narrator's performance and an inspiration for his further accomplishments. The narrator usually will address the male members of the gathering, but women are present too. The most appreciated are the tales about heroes (*vitezika paramisa*). These are also called long tales (*bare paramisa*) as some of them may last four or five hours. Sometimes they have to be continued the next day. A special occasion, when *bare paramisa* can be presented in their length, is at a wake for the dead which can take three days and nights.

Another genre of *paramisa* are short stories (*xarne*), which nearly always are funny (*pherasune*) and sometimes also dirty (*džungale*). While only a good *paramisaris* is able to tell a story lasting five hours, the short anecdotes are told by nearly everybody especially by young boys. If a *džungaľi paramisi* is told, children are always sent out from the room. While in formal gatherings the narrators are men, at home tales are told by women. For instance a mother-in-law will tell stories to her daughters-in-law while they are cooking, and a mother or grandmother to their children and grandchildren.

The types and motifs of Roma tales are sometimes unique – especially the way they are combined in the long tales – sometimes they are similar to other European tales, and some recognise Indian motifs as well. Roma tales have been collected for at least 150 years, often from dictation. These tales are summaries of the "real" long tales. Today, when folklorists have at their disposal tape recorders and video cameras, the traditional culture is rapidly disappearing.

Lovari storyteller Mihaly Rostas recounts a fairy tale to a participating audience in Nagyecsed in Hungary, near the border with Romania, in summer 1994.

The modern way of life, television addiction and the dispersal of Roma communities give less chance to continue with the wonderful storytelling tradition. However – as is the case of every developing nation – Romani literature may be gradually taking over the role and art of the traditional *paramisa*.

Romani songs

Roma attribute a high value to their songs. A *terňi bori* (young daughter-in-law) has to undergo several tests when she comes to the house of her *sasvi* (mother-in-law) and one of the tests is singing. If she sings well it may help her to avoid much of the harassment which every young *bori* has to suffer in the first years of her married life.

While at official cultural occasions the tales are performed by men, singing at the most formal function *bašaviben* (the playing of music connected with singing, dancing, drinking, eating) is performed by women. At *bašaviben* songs may fulfil a very important social role such as criticism or confession.

Criticism in songs

In the traditional Roma community it is not considered decent to criticise people directly. It would be considered offensive. However, all members of the community are at all times *tel e jakh* ("under the eye", under inspection, control) of others and anyone who does not behave according to *romipen* (norms of Roma culture) can be made aware of the social disapproval of his or her deviations. For example, the disapproval can be expressed indirectly through commonly accepted cultural forms. One of them is a song sung at a *bašaviben*. For instance if a man were to drink heavily and leave his wife and children without money, the wife would hire the woman who is the best singer in the community and she would sing in the presence of all Roma the complaint of the distressed wife. One song like that goes:

More, more, so tu keres	Oh man, what do you do
rati d'ives mato phires	you are drunk day and night
so zarodes, savoro prepijes	you spent in drinking all that you earn
aves khere la romňa mares	you come home and beat your wife

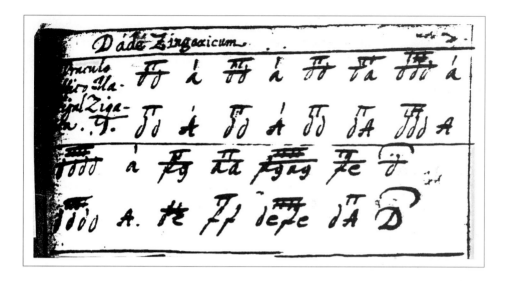

This song, with music, was the first to be written down in Romani in the 17th century. The meaning of the text is still not completely clear.

Songs of confession or repentance are also sung at the public *bašaviben*. If a man wanted to apologise to his wife or to express regret over his behaviour he would also have hired a singer who would sing his confession for him. For instance:

Devla, Devla, so me kerd'om,	Oh God, what did I do
mira dake e ladž kerd'om	I caused my mother to be ashamed
raňa romňa khere mukl'om	I left at home a gentle wife
lubňoraha svetos gejl'om	and I went away with a whore

Such songs belonged usually to the category of slow songs called *halgato*. In the Vlax community they are called *loke d'íla*.

However, a specific feature of the singing performance is that the same song begins by being sung as a *halgato* and after some time the singer shifts into *čardašis* (a dancing song). In the Vlax dialect – *khelimaski d'íli*. It may seem strange to non-Roma that a tragic text is expressed in a gay dancing melody. However, it is an effective metaphorical expression of an attitude towards life, or life-philosophy.

In the community of Servika Roma there is a special category of songs which are called *čorikane gil'a* (songs about being an orphan, being alone, deserted, poor, miserable). Some texts of such songs are very old. In the collection of the Polish folklorist Izidor Kopernicki who was collecting Romani songs in the second half of the nineteenth century are some songs which are still being sung today.

Marel o Del marel	God punishes
kas korkoro kamel	whom he himself wants
u man o Del mard'a	me also God has punished
na džanav vaš soske	I don't know why

Romani pop-music songs

Songs and singing are the most vivid part of Roma's folklore. Today new songs *(neve gil'a)* are being sung. The melodies are influenced by current pop-music. However, in the performance of even pop-music melodies there is always something very specifically Romani. Though many texts are influenced by pop-music cliches, many of them still continue the tradition which is expressed by a proverb: *e gili hin jekhfeder čačipen* (the song discloses the reality/truth, lit. "song is the best truth"). Unfortunately, the present situation makes Roma sing songs such as:

52

šele Romengero lav   The word of a hundred Roma
jekh gadžo prephagla.   can be "broken" by one gadžo
Soske o Rom pr'oda svetos   Why does Rom live in this world,
te les žadno patïv nane?   when he is not respected anywhere?

There are of course also more optimistic songs. There is an interesting new phenomenon. Many recent anonymous songs are appeals encouraging Roma to be aware of their ethnic identity, not to forget their language and not to imitate superficially the more prestigious gadžos.

Amen Roma sam, bisteras so sam,
gadžikenes, barikanes amen duma das.
Vaker Romanes, na gadžikanes,
ma ladža tut vaš tiri čhib romaňi

We are Roma, but we are forgetting who we are
we speak proudly the gadžo language.
Speak Romani, don't speak the gadžo language
don't be ashamed of your Romani language

Other genres

We have discussed the most popular and most formalised genres of Roma's folklore: the *paramisa* and the *giľa*. Still there are many other folklore genres: narratives of all kinds with themes such as the spirits of the dead (*mule*), witches (*čohaňa*) and dreams (*sune*). In each extended family stories about the ancestors are told again and again. It is very interesting for instance that even the representatives of the youngest generation can narrate in great detail the dramatic experiences of their grandfathers and great-grandfathers during the Second World War. Even stories from the First World War are still being told.

In the Kalderaš (or Kalderash) Roma community a specific narrative genre *divano* is popular. It is a description of some event, the aim of which is to evaluate (criticise) the situation, the behaviour of the agents of the event, etc. This sort of narrative has one important function of a "social corrective", or current reproduction and communication of the ethic norms, of *romipen*.

Proverbs and riddles

Like every nation, Roma also appreciate the *goďaver lava* (wise words / opinions) preserved in proverbs and several relating to language are used in this book. Also, because *dživipen džal lokeder pherasenca* (life goes forward more easily with jokes), joking and riddles are very popular. You may try your wit and guess the answer to some traditional riddles on the next page.

Romani language games

A specific category of riddles are language games *"sar pes phenel – s'oda hin?"* (how do you say? – what does it mean?) Language games are very popular which shows that Roma are interested in their language and its development or "purity". The way they are played is very simple. Somebody asks the other participant(s) how they would translate into Romani some word or phrase which is not common. His/her challenge is opened by the question *sar pes phenel?* (how do you say?) The "truest", "purest" Romani word is appreciated the best – and the reward of the "winner" is his satisfaction that he is a *čačo Rom* (real, true Rom) because among the required qualities of a *čačo Rom* proficiency in Romani is valued, as is his or her ability to use beautiful words *(šukar lava)*. In recent years the Servika Roma from the Czech Republic like to test each other with neologisms like *genďi* (book, derived from *genel* "to read"), *čitro* "picture" (an Indic-based neologism), *luludi* "flower" (adopted from the Vlax dialect instead of the Czech loanword *kvitkos*), *luma* "world" (adopted from Vlax dialect, instead of the Czech *svetos*), etc.

Try to say quickly ten times:

Lel len? Na lel len.

Does he take them? He doesn't take them

If the participants are challenged to translate some *čačo romano lav* (real Romani word) into the gadžo language the introductory question is *s'oda hin?* what does it mean? Such "real" words are usually either archaic terms which the one who puts the question has heard from his ancestors, or terms from other Romani dialects, or also neologisms acquired from Romani written texts,

Romani riddles

Hin man ajso čhavo, teďol calo rat andro pañi, cindo nane
I have a son who is standing the whole night in the water and does not get wet

(Answer: o Čhon – the moon)

So keras savore džene jekhetane?
What do all of us do at the same moment?

(Answer: phuruvas – we are getting old)

So kerel čhavoro, kana uľol?
What does a child do when it gets born?

(Answer: kerel than avre čhavoreske andre la dakero per – it makes room for another child in the womb of his mother)

Jekh kaľi andro kalo veš
parne čhave šel the deš
pijel loľi mol
šoha na maťol

She is a black one in a black forest
she has hundred and ten white children
she is drinking red wine
and she never gets drunk

(Answer: e džuv – a louse)

čhinel sar čhuri,
sasťarel o jilo,
anel tut pro lačho drom,
šaj tut marel pal o drom tele

It can cut like a knife
it can cure the heart
it can take you on the right way
and it can take you away from the right way

(Answer: o lav – the word)

books or journals. Popular test-words are *šošoj* "hare", *sir* "garlic", *diz* "castle" and *bešťi* "chair". These words have conserved their Indic forms only in some regional varieties of Servika Romani, but otherwise they are replaced by the Slovak loanwords.

Sometimes bets are taken in riddle games and the winner takes all as prize money. This makes the game even more interesting but it is not a rule and Roma enjoy riddle and language-riddle games even without financial rewards.

IV. Language and culture

In this chapter we will discuss a number of cultural traits which are reflected in language. We will deal with the names that Roma use to describe and to define themselves and others, both Roma and non-Roma. Further we will discuss some religious and cultural terms. We will also discuss family names and first names, both official ones and the names which Roma use only among themselves. The names that Roma have for themselves and other Roma groups are complex. There are terms used by outsiders for Roma, and there are terms the Roma use for themselves. Roma often have distinct names for their own group and names for other Roma groups, and also distinct names for non-Roma.

What do Gypsies call themselves?

"Rom", or in plural "Roma", is the main universal ethnic group name, which is used by most of the Romani groups in the world. As pointed out in Chapter II, an Indian sound Ḍ like the 'd' in the Indian pronunciation of *pappadam* has changed to a form of 'r' in Romani. Therefore there is possibly an etymological link between the name Roma and the Indian caste name Ḍom.

The word "Roma" must have been the original name of all the European Gypsies, even though not all of them call themselves Roma today. There are also groups who call themselves Kalo, Manuš, Romano, Romanichal or Sinti. For unknown reasons, these people seem to have lost the original group name "Roma". The alternative scenario, which would claim that they never had it, is less likely. Even though "Rom(a)" is not used for the ethnic group by these groups of Gypsies, they nevertheless call their language *Romanes*, exactly the same as those people who call themselves "Roma". This means literally "in the manner of the Gypsies", or they say *Romani čhib* "the Romani tongue". The language of the Kalo, Manuš, Romanichal and Sinti is moreover demonstrably the same as the language of the Roma.

The *Sinti* are Gypsies who live in Austria, Belgium, Germany, Eastern France, Northern Italy, and the Netherlands, with some scattered groups in the Czech Republic, Hungary, Russia and elsewhere. The origin of the name *Sinti* (plural; the singular form is *Sinto* for a man and *Sinta* or *Sintitsa* for a woman) by which they call themselves is not clear. They usually call their language *Romanes*, but some groups also use the word *Sinto* or *Sintitikes*.

In France there are people who call themselves *Manuš* (or *Manouche*). This is a Romani word meaning "human being, man". They speak basically the same variety of the language as the *Sinti*.

In areas as far apart as Spain, Wales and Finland the Gypsy groups call themselves *Kalé* (plural, in singular *Kalo* for a man and *Kali* for a woman). This name is taken from the common Romani word *kalo* which means "black", and formerly it was also used in other parts of Europe as well with the meaning "Gypsy".

English Gypsies call themselves *Romanichal*, but many of them also use the English name "Gypsy". This name is or was also used in the Basque Country, France, Germany and Scandinavia. The first part of the word is of course the same as the adjective *Romani* "of the Roma", but the origin of the second part *-chal* is unclear.

These are all names these groups use for themselves – which may or may not include other Gypsies. Roma often also have names for other Roma groups, to which they feel they do not belong themselves. Often these relate to a country of origin. For instance, among the Baltic Roma the derogatory term *Xaraóny (Faraóny)* "Pharaohs" is used for other Roma.

What do outsiders call Gypsies?

The Roma are mostly known under other names by non-Roma. The two most widespread names used by outsiders for Gypsies are based on two different roots. The first of these is the word *Egyptian*, in whatever the local language happens to be, and the other is perhaps derived from *athinganoi* or *asingar*.

The local word for Egyptian led to names like *Gitano* in Spain, *Gitan* in France, and *Gypsy* in English. This term is very old. It dates from the earliest period when the first groups of Roma arriving in Europe claimed to be noblemen from Egypt or Little Egypt. Some places where early Roma lived were called "Little Egypt". This was either a settlement in the Byzantine Empire in what is now Greece but could be a general term for the Middle East.

The other common name for Gypsies used by outsiders led to names like *Zigeuner* in Germany, the Netherlands and Scandinavia, *Tsigane* in France, *Ţigan* in Romania, *Çingene* in Turkey, *Zingaro* and *Zigano* in Italy, *Cigano* in Portugal, *Cigán* in Czech and other Slavic languages. There are two theories on the origin of this name. Some think that it is derived from an Iranian term for the trade of blacksmith – an occupation followed by men in many Roma groups. A Kurdish (Iranian) word for blacksmith is *asingar*. Other people think it may be derived from the historical term *athingani*, used to describe people who were considered heretics by the Orthodox church in south-eastern Europe. They were originally from the eastern part of the Byzantine Empire and had moved to the western part. Perhaps the Roma were identified with them because both Roma and *athingani* were foreigners from the east, with different languages and customs. Perhaps the Roma themselves were *athingani* or vice versa.

Both terms have acquired a pejorative meaning in the course of time. To a speaker of Czech and Slovak, the terms *Cikán* and *Cigán* evoke a picture of a dirty, dishevelled creature. In Slovak the verb *cigánit* means "to lie". Such negative connotations disparaging Roma have developed as a result of centuries of misunderstanding between Roma and majority societies. In English, the term *Gypsy* is often used as a synonym for "wanderer" but many groups of Roma, certainly in Central and Eastern Europe, have been housedwellers for three or four centuries. In fact, the ancestors of some Roma endured centuries of slavery, and with it forced settlement, and paradoxically the descendants of these people became prototypical nomads in the West.

What do Gypsies want to be called?

In many countries, Gypsies prefer to be called by the name they use to refer to themselves: Roma, Sinti and the like. This wish has been expressed on numerous occasions by the political associations set up by Gypsies. It also appears in the names of these associations, e.g. International Romani Union, Verband Deutscher Sinti, etc.

Many countries promoting respect for minority rights, at a formal level at any rate, have adopted the name "Roma", or "Roma and Sinti" for use in official contexts. The Romanian government, however, refused to adopt it because, it was said, the name Roma is too similar to the name of their country. The Romanian authorities therefore continue to use the pejorative term *ţigan*.

Some people use the word Romanies in English, to cover all people who speak the Romani language, because even those Gypsies who call themselves Kalé, Romanichals and Sinti use the words Romano, Romani and Romanes to describe their culture and ethnic identity.

By what names are Romani groups called?

The Romani community is divided into different subgroups, by language, occupation and so on. The main distinction that Roma make in many areas is on the basis of occupation. This may be an inheritance from the caste system of India, from where the ancestors of the Roma came. In India, a person is born into a certain caste defined by the type of work the members do. One cannot leave the caste into which one is born. The caste, called *jati* in India, is thus both a kinship and professional group.

In Romani communities, subgroup boundaries follow the distinctions between the occupations, and these also correspond with kinship differentiation. People marry within their own group, but not those with whom they have close blood ties. Many subgroups of Roma call themselves by occupational terms. These are only rarely of Romani origin. Some examples are *Kalderash* or *Kalderari* "coppersmiths, kettle smiths" (from Romanian *caldera* "kettle"), *Lovara* "horse dealers" (from Hungarian *ló* "horse"), *bugurdži* "driller, drill maker" (from Turkish *burgucu* "drill maker"). There are many subgroups and not all of them can be listed here.

The naming of these subgroups can be very complicated. Names based on occupations are often regional. For instance the term *Ursari* (from Romanian *ursi* "bear") is used for bear leaders in Moldova, Romania, Ukraine, and elsewhere, but in Slovakia they are called *Medvedara* (from Slovak *medved'* "bear") or *ričkara* (from Romani *rič* "bear", like in Hindi *rič*). In Turkey they are called *Ajdžijes* (from Turkish *ayı* "bear" and in the Balkans often *Mečkara* (from Slav *mečka* "bear"). Even if these names describe the same occupation, the groups concerned do not necessarily recognise each other as being somehow "the same", nor do they necessarily speak the same dialect of Romani.

It should also be noted that these occupational terms may be more historical than contemporary reflections of their occupations: today, people calling themselves "Lovara" often do work which does not involve horses at all.

Apart from these occupational terms, Romani groups may be named after a country or region with which they were associated before they migrated to their current place of residence. For instance in Argentina a group of Roma who came from the former Soviet Union are called *Rusurja* "Russians". Similarly, the term *Vlax Roma* is a term derived from the name *Wallachia*, a Slavic term for Romania. The ancestors of this group lived there for a long time and they have many Romanian loanwords in their dialect. Vlax Roma in the Czech and Slovak Republics have coined the appellation *Romungri* (from *Rom Ungro* "Hungarian Roma") for the Romani groups who have been settled in the area for centuries and who apparently came there from Hungary.

Unlike group names describing occupations, these regional names are mostly formed and used by others, and may be felt as insults. As one Romungro puts it: "If you say *Poják* to a Vlax Rom – as we call them – he will hit you".

Regional names may also describe the landscape in which a given group lives. In Poland for instance, there are groups called *Bergitka Roma* or *Cyganie wyżynni* "Roma of the mountains", *Felditka Roma* or *Nizinni*, "Roma of the plains" and *Vešitka Roma* or *Lešaki* "Roma of the forest". *Vešitka Roma* are also found in Russia.

Just to be clear: these occupational and regional names denote subgroups. They use "Roma" as the general term and "Romanes" for their language.

Not all Roma use regional or occupational group names

Not all Roma use regional or occupational group names. Some Roma in the Balkans and quite a few of the Roma in Central Europe call themselves simply Roma, or *čače Roma* "the true, real Roma". Many groups feel that they are somehow "the best", and so is their variety of Romani. Most groups in southern, northern and western Europe and the northern part of Central Europe never use occupational terms. Those are mostly limited to speakers of the so-called Vlax and Balkan dialects.

What terms do linguists and other scholars use?

Today, mostly terms like Roma and Sinti are used in academic writing, as well as the names of the occupational subgroups. Linguists have also created special words to describe groups or related dialects. For example the term Carpathian Romani is used to describe Roma living in this region of Central Europe. This term, however, is not used by, or even known by, the groups it covers. The same is true for terms like "Northern dialects" or "Central dialects": these are scholarly terms not used by most Roma.

Names by which the Roma call non-Roma

The Roma have names not only for themselves and other Romani groups, but also for all non-Roma, and sometimes for particular subgroups of non-Roma. These terms differ slightly from area to area.

The term *Gadžo, Gažo* or in England *Gaujo/Gorgio*, is the most common term denoting anybody who is not a Rom. Its etymology is not certain, but it may derive from an Indian word meaning "villager, born in a village" (Sanskrit or Old Indic *gramdža*, or in the modern language Marvari of India *gavdžo*).

The term *Goro* is not as common as *Gadžo*. It is probably related to the word *gora/goro* in Hindi, which means a person with a fair complexion. In some varieties of *Servika Romani* the term *gadžo* is only used for non-Roma villagers while *goro* is a general term for non-Roma.

The word *Das(o)* is used in many Balkan dialects for Christian non-Rom, whereas *Xoraxano* is used for the Muslims in the Balkans, often more specifically Turks or sometimes Albanians. It is also used by Roma groups, for themselves or for others, as a name for Muslim Roma in the Balkans. In some Romani dialects (e.g. Iran, Wales) the same term simply means "foreigner". Its etymology is possibly the word *Qor'an* "Koran", or more specifically "Qor'an reader". The etymology of *Das* is probably an Indian word for "slave", in analogy to words like "Slav" and "Serb" for these groups.

The word *xalo* is fairly widespread and is often somewhat 'slangy'. It may come from the Romani root *xalo* "bald or bad person" or from *xa-* meaning "to eat", perhaps "one who wants to eat a lot, a stingy or silly person". Less common names include *Buzno* (Ukraine, Spain), derived from the Romani word for "goat", [*Buro* in Germany (from an old Germanic word for farmer)] and *Balamo* in Greece and Turkey, of unknown origin. A few additional terms are strictly regional, such as *Payo* in Spain or *Tsitsalo* in the Baltic area. In Ungriko Romani the term *prosto* is used for a non-Rom. Its etymology is the Slavic word for "simple".

For people of African origin Romani speakers may use *Kalo* or *Kaljardo*, from the Romani word for "black". This same word is also used as a name for themselves by some Roma groups (see above p. 58).

From this list it is clear that the Roma are like the Gadže in their naming behaviour. They use one term to generalise over all those who do not belong to their group, ignoring the diversity of the Gadže. Most of the terms used by Roma for non-Roma "outsiders" are unflattering, negative and belittling. Here again, they do not differ from Gadže. This may also be the case for some of the terms relating to other Roma groups, just like many Europeans have nicknames for neighbouring nations.

Surnames

The Roma usually have surnames common to the non-Roma among whom they live. For instance typical Romani surnames in England are Boswell, Lee and Smith. Stoika is one of the most typical Lovari surnames. East European Kalderash are often called Demeter while in Sweden the Taikons prevail. The name Horvath is also common, both among Roma and non-Roma.

Maria Theresa, Empress of the Austro-Hungarian empire in the eighteenth century, forced Roma to change their names. Nevertheless, some Indian-based Romani surnames have been preserved. Some of these are: *Kaleja* (Romani: *kaleja!* "hey black one!"), *Thuleja* (Romani: *thuleja!* "hey fat one!"). Some other surnames are reminiscent of Indian caste names, such as Badi, Badžo, Džugi, and others. *Badi* is a sub-caste of Dom musicians, and so is *Badža* (the Hindi word *badžana* means "to play"). *Džugi* is a sub-caste of mendicant yogis.

First names

Most Roma use two kinds of names. First, they have an official name which is "in their passport". This is their *gadžikano nav*, or "Gadžo name". Second, they also have a *Romano nav* "Romani name", the main function of which is to protect the individual. The protective name must be different from the official passport name. In some communities the *Romano nav* is also called *aver nav* "the other name". A Romani political leader from the Czech Republic is officially called

63

Jan but no Rom knows him under this name because his *Romano nav* is Lad'a.

The *Romano nav* may be a current Christian or Muslim name, but it is usually more colourful than a "passport" name. It may be derived from some salient physical feature or personal quality, e.g. *Kalo* "black", *Vuštval'i* "fat-lipped", *čikňi* "little", *Papin* "goose", *čhibal'i* "backbiting", *Pušumori* "little flea" (i.e. as quick as a flea).

Names taken from television programmes are also favourite, such as *Sandokan*, *Angelika*, *Vinetu* and *Olčetrhen* (Old Shatterhand). The names of famous politicians can be found in Romani communities as well: *Klinton*, *Jeltsin*, *Gandi* and *Stalin*.

Creativity in the coining of a *Romano nav* is unlimited. These names may change over time, be replaced or added. Over the course of his life the journalist Gejza D. from the Czech Republic was known variously as *Tonču* (Anthony), *Kalo* (black), *Buxlo Nakh* (Broad nose) and *Majpejl'omas* "I nearly fell over".

Place names

Most Romani speakers call places by their local names, adjusted to the sound patterns of Romani. They would say, for instance, Amsterdamo for Amsterdam, while Buenos Aires is called Bunozaria in Romani.

Place names may also be translated. Roma who live in the Turkish city Kırk Ağac call it Saranda Rukha, a literal translation of the Turkish name which means "forty trees". Translation is also found on other levels. The Slovak place name Lomnička, for instance, is a diminutive form of Lomnica; Roma call this town Cikňi Lomňica, literally "Little Lomnica".

In some areas the Roma use place names which are quite different from the "official" ones, often because they come from an area where a different place name was used, or because they spoke a language of a local minority rather than the national language. Vienna, for instance, is called by its Hungarian name Beči in Romani. Some Roma groups in Slovakia use Hungarian place names rather than the Slovak ones, following the usages of the local Hungarian-speaking minority.

Another interesting aspect of Romani place names is what Roma call the communities where they themselves live. In most East and Central European countries many Roma live in neighbourhoods separate from non-Roma. In the Balkans these are called *mahalla*, after the Turkish word for "neighbourhood".

In Slovakia other terms are used, such as *khera* "houses", *thana* "places", *heličke* "places" (a Hungarian word) or even *xara* "holes".

Only in a limited number of Romani groups, primarily those who came into Western Europe in the 15th century, do we find place names actually translated into Romani. The translation may be literal: the town Welshpool, for instance, is *Wåľšenengi Pani* "water of the Welsh" in the local Romani, In Abruzzi Romani the name *Tširiklí* (Romani *tširiklo/ tširikli* "bird") is used for Monte Falcone, literally "Falcon Mountain". In Spain the Romani town name *Gao Parné* is a literal translation of its Spanish name Villa Blanca "white town". In some cases puns are used. "Beans" are *boba* in Romani and *hava* is Spanish for "beans" so that Gitanos (Gypsies in Spain) use *Bobana* for "Havana". Most of these examples are exceptions. In general, Roma use place names that are also used by the local population.

Some Romani kinship terms

The most important social unit for the Roma is the extended family, which comprises three to five generations. Their members support each other (*l'ikeren/ikren pe(s)*) in the spirit of family identity.

The family is called *famelia*, and some dialects use other terms such as *čalado*, *endaňi* (Ungriko group in Hungary) *akraba* (Xoraxani group; Muslim Roma in the Balkans) or *semja* (Baltic Romani). In Servika Romani the expression *romňi čhave* "wife children" is used. Even though the terms may differ, the content and cultural value is the same.

The members of the family are: *dad* "father", *daj* or *dej* "mother", *čhavo* or *šavo* "son", *čhaj* or *šej* "daughter", *phral* "brother" (in some dialects this also means first cousin), *phen* "sister", *papu(s)* "grandfather", *baba* or *mami* "grandmother", *kako, ujcus, bačis* "uncle", *bibi/tsetka/nena/lala* "aunt", *rom* "husband", *romni* "wife", *džamutro* "son in law", *bori* "daughter in law" or "sister in law", *sastro* "father in law", *sasvi/sasuj* "mother in law". In some Romani varieties different terms may be used as well, or precise collocations are used such as *le dadeskere phraleskero čhavo*, literally "the son of father's brother", for a cousin.

Typically, Romani uses other terms for children of non-Roma. Whereas *čhave* or *čhavore* can be used for all kinds of children, the words *rakli* "daughter, girl" and *raklo* "son, boy" can only be used for non-Roma.

Terms for traditional institutions

Many Roma groups have complex kinship or clan systems. Groups like the Lovari or Kalderash consist of what are called *vitsi* and *fajta*. These are clans or lineages and can be reckoned from the mother's or father's side. In Russia and some other parts of the former Soviet Union the word *irí* is used to denote a clan.

The *natsia* is a bigger unit again, used among the Vlax Roma, covering a number of *vitsi*. Not all Roma groups have an equivalent for this unit, and in other dialects it just means *nation*.

The term *kumpania* refers to a social unit of (formerly nomadic) Roma who travel(led) and live(d) together. Vlax groups such as the Lovari and Kalderash have these kumpanias. The sedentary Roma of Slovakia use various other terms for groupings in their settlements, such as *amare xara/khera/thana/helički* "our holes/houses/ places/places", where *amare* can be replaced by *Romane*. Sometimes loanwords such as *taboris/vatra/kolonia* are used. The term *irí* is used by Russian Xaladytka Roma for "family tree" and *sementsa* in all Baltic groups for "relatives".

The term *kher* means "house". It is also used for "flat, room" and its secondary meaning also covers "household", whereas other groups use *cerha* "tent" for "household".

Terms for important persons and events

Baptism (*bolipen*, some dialects *boňa, keresteliśígo*) takes place among Christian Roma. The service of a *raśaj* "priest" is demanded. This is not necessary for the marriage (*bijav, abijau*). A burial (*praxomo*, dialectal *paruśagos*) is preceded by a wake. Funeral rites are important to prevent the spirit of the deceased (*mulo*) from coming back and frightening the living relatives. Here too, the service of a priest is needed.

The term *Romimo/Romipen/Romanipen* "Romani tradition, law, Romness" is an important word which symbolises the identity of Roma, extending beyond the group or clan boundaries. It covers law, culture, habits, tradition, behaviour, language and all the positive values shared by Roma. The opposition *pat'iv* "respect, honour" versus *ladž/lažavo* "shame" regulates the behaviour of the members of the Romani community.

Many groups have their own systems of justice. Some turn to elders or a council of elders. Groups like Lovari and Kalderash have an institutional trial called *kris(i)*. A group of *krisara* "judges" headed by an *angluno Rom* "first/foremost Rom, president" decide on violations of the *Romimo*. The most severe punishment is excommunication from the group for a period of time. This period corresponds with the severity of the crime.

Religious terms

The word *Del* or *Devel* "God" is the central term in the faith of the Roma. Sometimes attributes are used, such as *Baro Del* "Great God" and *Gulo Del* "Sweet God". In addressing God the pronoun *mro* or *mo* "my" is often used, and there is a special term when addressing God: *Devla* "Oh God!"

God is also the major power referred to in blessings and curses: *O Del tuke te šegitenel* "May God help you" or *Mi del o Del lačho d'ives* "May God give you a good day", *O Del tut te arakhel* "May God protect you". Sentences like *thovav tut le Devleske* "I hand you over to God" show that final justice is in the hands of God. God is the only and the greatest universal power and all good or evil powers or beings are only instruments through which He acts.

Roma are often reproached for not attending church. For Roma it is more important to show respect for God individually and to live a good life, than to worship in churches or mosques. A Romani proverb is *Miri khangeri hin miro jilo* "My church is my heart".

The concept of prayer is expressed by phrases like *mangel le Devles* "to ask God", *ašarel le Devles* "to praise God" and *cirdel pharo vod'i kijo Del* "to sigh to God". Prayers are often individual conversations with God, and these may also be expressed in songs, because: *Andro gil'a vakeren o Roma le Devleha* "It is in songs that Roma talk to God".

The devil, *O Beng*, is a negative being. Sometimes a different term is used, such as *bižužo* "impure", *nalačho* "bad" because: *phenes beng, o beng pes tuke sikhavla* "If you say 'devil', the devil will appear".

Diseases are not called by their names but often euphemistic terms are used, e.g. *džungalo nasval'ipen* "bad illness" for "syphilis" or "cancer", or *šuko nasval'ipen* for "tuberculosis".

A common belief among the Roma is that of the *mulo*. This spirit of the dead reappears to living people to help, advise or warn, if these are good; the mulo is usually one of the ancestors. He may also punish them if they owe him something, or if they were not good to him while he was alive. For this reason most Roma do not speak about deceased persons and do not carry their pictures. In some cases the possessions of the deceased are burnt soon after his or her death.

A *rašaj* "priest" has the important function of performing various rites such as baptism or exorcising the intrusive *mulo*.

There is much potential confusion about names for different Gypsy groups. In addition the terms used in different domains reflect the various cultures of the Roma.

V. Unity and diversity

This chapter discusses dialects of Romani and the influence of Romani on other languages. It also examines more deeply the distinction between Romani and the speech forms of Travellers, and Romani and Para-Romani.

Where is Romani spoken?

Romani is spoken in all European countries except Iceland and maybe Portugal. There are many more speakers in Central and Eastern Europe than in Western Europe. Romani is also spoken outside Europe, especially in Americas, Australia and South Africa. It is probably the most widespread language of the European community.

Do all Roma understand one another?

To a certain extent all Roma understand one another. Nevertheless, in some cases the understanding can be limited as the language has changed in different directions in different areas. The Romani communities spread through Europe from the early fifteenth century after which they were not in contact. This is comparable with the difficulties a modern English speaker can have understanding Shakespeare (around 1600 AD) or Chaucer (around 1400 AD). English, however, has changed more significantly than Romani has since 1400.

Are there dialects of Romani?

As in any language, there are dialects in the Romani language but is not possible to give an exact number. Some scholars mention 60 dialects but that is an arbitrary number. It is often difficult or impossible to say where one dialect ends and another begins.

It is certain that there was already dialectal variation in Romani at the time of the arrival of the Roma in Europe. Since then different clans have developed separate features that may or may not have been present in the original dialects. In particular the dialects of sedentary Roma have also been affected by the languages of the majority population where they live. As a consequence there are many dialects. The differences, however, may not be greater than the dialect variation of, say, English. Some of the dialects of Romani are given here:

This map shows the major dialect divisions of Romani according to scholars.

A. Dialects spoken in one area:

- Erli and Arli of the Balkans (Bulgaria, Greece, Yugoslavia). Speakers of these dialects from the Balkans can be found in most countries of western Europe. They migrated to the west mostly from the 1960s (570,000 speakers).
- Balto-Slavic dialects: the dialects of the Baltic states, Belarus, Poland and Russia (500,000 speakers).
- Slovak/Servika Romani, in the Czech Republic and Slovakia (500,000).
- Romungro, in Hungary, South Poland and South Slovakia. Also called Carpathian (40,000).
- Sinti-Manouche, spoken in Belgium, France, Germany and Holland and North Italy by an unknown number of people.
- Ungriko, spoken in the Czech Republic and Slovakia.
- Xoraxano, a group of dialects spoken by Muslim Roma from the Balkans.

There are numerous minor local dialects, such as Kalo of Finland, Abruzzi and Calabria Romani in South Italy, each with a few thousand speakers.

B. Dialects spoken in scattered places:

- Kalderash, Lovari, Churari and other dialects are spoken by descendants of former slaves in Romania. These people dispersed through Europe and the Americas after the abolition of slavery from around the middle of the last century. These dialects are also spoken in Hungary and Romania, from where they originate. More than one million people speak these dialects.
- other dialects of former nomads spoken in scattered places in the Balkans and more recently also in Western Europe, such as the dialect of the *Sepedži* (basket-makers) of Shumen, Bulgaria (110,000).

Scholars divide these dialects into four main groupings roughly equally four regional areas (see the map on page 70).

The so-called Northern dialects cover most of northern, western and southern Europe, most of Poland, Russia and the Baltic states (e.g. Balto-Slavic dialects, Sinti-Manouche, South Italy, Finland). Some of the Northern dialects of the westernmost area evolved into forms of Para-Romani (see below).

The Central dialects are spoken from south Poland to Hungary and from eastern Austria to the Ukraine (e.g. Servika/Slovak Romani, Romungro, Ungriko).

The Balkan dialects are spoken in the Balkans and Turkey (e.g. Erli, Arli, Xoraxano).

The Vlax dialects just about everywhere but originally in what is now Romania and Hungary (e.g. Churari, Kalderash, Lovari).

In all cases it is clearly the same language.

How do Romani dialects differ?

All Romani dialects have basically the same words for everyday items such as body parts, kinship terms, food, common activities, feelings, numbers, natural phenomena and common animals. They usually have different words for for technical items, non-traditional jobs and the like.

The more technical vocabulary, including subjects learned about in schools rather than at home, is often from another language. In the Vlax dialects that language is Rumanian, in Balkan dialects it is Slavic or Turkish, and in Central dialects Hungarian, to which words from the languages of the current location are also added.

The grammatical system also differs somewhat from one dialect to the next. For instance, for "you are" some people say "hal" (Central dialects, Sinti), others say "san". The word for "I am" can be *sem* (Vlax dialects), *som* or *sum* (most Balkan dialects), or *hum* (Sinti dialect).

Is Romani a "jargon" or a form of "cant"?

Romani is not a jargon, and it is not used mainly by Travellers. We have already discussed the position of Romani as the native language of the community of people called Roma, and we have dealt with the origins and everyday functions of the language. However, there are indeed connections between the Romani language and the forms of speech used by travelling populations. These forms are often called "cant" or "jargon", both by outsiders and many speakers. In order to clarify and explain these connections, we need firstly to define in more detail than above what we mean by "jargon" or "cant".

When talking about "cant" or "jargon" we are not attempting to attach a value to any form of speech, in the sense that this speech form should be considered as "bad" or "inappropriate" language. "Jargon" in the strictly linguistic sense is not at all "bad" or "decayed" speech; what it is, rather, is a vocabulary that is used by a particular group of people, in particular situations and by conscious choice rather than as a natural and everyday language. This is also true for "cant". Jargons consist mainly of vocabulary words; they usually have no grammar and no accent of their own. In the strictly linguistic sense, they are not, therefore, distinct languages, but rather sets of words that can be inserted into general speech.

As in all languages, there are dialect differences in Romani as well, but basic communication is always possible between Romani speakers from all parts of the world. This sentence means: "I love you" in varieties from Southeastern and Northern Europe.

There are at least two types of jargons. One is specialised professional jargon which consists of the technical vocabulary used by members of a particular profession: land surveyors, lawyers, masons, surgeons and so on. These words cover concepts that are of direct and everyday importance only to those people who practise that particular trade. In other words, knowledge of the jargon is connected to the specialised knowledge of the profession. Romani does not usually play a role in this type of jargon.

The other type of jargon is often referred to as a "secret language" or an "in-group language". It is not a professional vocabulary; rather, it includes words for everyday concepts such as food and drink, buying and selling, persons and animals, numbers and so on. This type of jargon is usually used by entire communities that share cultural and religious customs. Its speakers may engage in similar occupations, based either on trade or providing services as artisans, craftsmen or entertainers. In particular, families who are engaged in trades that require travelling – such as work at fairs, circuses, arts and crafts markets, etc. – will share a very close-knit working and living environment and are likely to develop and use their own in-group jargons.

These in-group forms of speech can help reinforce and emphasise membership in the group, just like the fashionable slang expressions teenagers will use on occasions within their circle of close friends. This is one function. Another important function of jargons is to allow group members to communicate secretly in the presence of strangers who are not group members. This secretive function of jargons developed during a time in which many travelling and professional groups were outlawed or persecuted and needed to keep their messages, and often their mere identity, secret. Many traders also use jargon to negotiate transactions when they do not wish to be understood by their customers or competitors. Finally, Travellers who reside in caravans on campsites have often needed to rely on such forms of speech for secret communication in situations where they were threatened by eviction.

Roma and Travellers, Romani and jargons

Many Roma specialised in what we could call "travelling" or "nomadic" occupations. As an immigrant minority in western Europe, the Roma found a market for their crafts and artisan skills. From the eighteenth century onwards permanent settlements became the rule for most Roma but many continued to engage in travelling occupations. They would leave their settlements for certain periods of time and reside in campsites while working at fairs or markets or selling goods and services in remote areas, hence many Roma came into contact with the travelling populations which we mentioned above.

The Roma always had a language of their own. They did not need to invent a jargon because their everyday language, Romani, was foreign and incomprehensible to outsiders anyway. For Roma who were engaged in travelling occupations and who often lived on campsites, Romani was not only their everyday language, it also served as a secret language, just like the jargons of non-Romani Travellers.

Picture the recurring encounters between Romani and non-Romani Travellers: In the first, the Roma had a language of their own. In the second, the Travellers of non-Romani origin, often used a jargon for special purposes such as those we highlighted above: in-group and secret communication. Since jargons are in need of new words that would not be understood by the majority population outside the Traveller communities, they often looked to the Romani language as a source of vocabulary.

All over Europe are jargons that have absorbed Romani words. The number of those words varies considerably. The number of words taken from Romani that they contain range from none at all to several hundreds. In some jargons, such as those of the Jenisch Travellers in southern Germany, up to one third of the vocabulary can derive from Romani. Other sources for words include French, local German dialects, Hebrew, Italian, Latin, and "disguise" certain strategies. Many dozen Romani-derived words are also found in some Czech, French, Hungarian, Italian, Romanian and jargons, as well as elsewhere.

There are even some jargons that are almost entirely based on Romani vocabulary. That is, there are travelling groups who are not Romani speaking, but who, among themselves, use the language of the country in which they live, such as Norwegian or Swedish. Then, as an in-group form of speech they will insert words derived almost entirely from Romani into their speech. It is possible or even likely that these groups are descendants of Romani Travellers who have stopped using the Romani language. They would have kept a vocabulary derived from it, which they now use as an in-group jargon. We find such Romani-based jargons in various countries and regions in Europe.

Romani words in several types of slang – and standard English

Romani has not only influenced Traveller speech, but also different kinds of slang and cant and even some standard languages. Slang words of Romani origin were adopted via Travellers' speech or directly from Roma, in towns and villages where Roma formed a significant part of the population. Romanian slang, for example, is known to have a great many words of Romani origin. One that is well known and widely used is *mishto* meaning "good". Swedish slang, especially that used in the capital city Stockholm, also has many Romani-derived items; the word *chay* for "girl" is one that is by now in common use in spoken Swedish. Spanish slang also abounds in Romani words, and even dictionaries will list a word like *gache* for "fellow, guy", derived from the Romani word *gadžo*, in the plural *gadže*, meaning a person of non-Romani origin. Further examples of common Romani words found in slang are the following in Italian *gergo* (cant): *čiri(no)* "knife" (Romani *čhuri*), *grai* "horse", *kakaña* "chicken" (Romani *kahni*), *lovi* "money" (Romani *lové*), *muj* "face". In German only a few Romani words have entered more popular usage, one of them is *Zaster* meaning "money", from the Romani word *saster* originally meaning "iron" or "metal" (used in jargons as a sort of code word for a metal coin).

English slang has also adopted Romani words, such as *div* and *pani*. Some Romani words, such as *lollipop* (from Romani *loli phabai* "red apple") and *cosh "stick"*, have come into common usage. Finally, we should of course mention the English word *pal*, from Romani *phral* meaning "brother", which is probably the most widely known word in English originating from the Romani language.

Mixed forms of speech that are based on Romani

In some communities that identify themselves as Gypsies or Travellers, forms of speech are used that have similarities with Romani. Their speakers may even refer to them as "Romany", as do Travellers in England and Sweden, or they may have a special name for their language, as in the case of the "Caló" speech of Spanish and Portuguese Gypsies. These speech forms are different from Romani in that they are essentially forms of the majority language of the country (for example English, Spanish or Swedish) but include words that derive from Romani. Usually, such speech forms are used in encounters within the Gypsy or Traveller community. They may be used to emphasise the membership in the group, or to establish the membership in the group of unfamiliar people: if you speak the language, you must be a member. Sometimes, they are also used by Gypsies and Travellers as a secret language to prevent outsiders from understanding what they are saying.

It is clear that these speech forms are not, strictly speaking, dialects of Romani, since only their vocabulary is taken from the Romani language, but not their grammar or pronunciation. At the same time they do share a great many words with Romani. Their speakers often consider them to be separate languages, that are closer to Romani than to the majority language (English, Swedish, etc.).

There is disagreement among linguists as to how exactly these speech varieties came into being. It seems to have been an act of ingenious creativity which would have enabled these Gypsies to shift to the country's language while preserving Romani to a great extent. Some regard these varieties as the product of mixed marriages between Roma and non-Roma, whose descendants created a mixed language. Others consider them as traces of Romani dialects that had once been spoken in Gypsy communities but were gradually forgotten and replaced by the majority language, although a Romani-based vocabulary was still retained. Typically we find Para-Romani in those areas where Romani (with Indic endings) has been lost. It is also unclear whether mixed varieties based on Romani were once used as everyday languages by the community since nowadays they appear to be confined to occasional single utterances, and the Romani vocabulary is learned only in adolescence when children begin to participate in the family's economic activities. These mixed forms are sometimes called Para-Romani, since they are clearly related to Romani but they have become different languages.

Para-Romani

In some areas Romani has been replaced by so-called Para-Romani languages, which preserve only the Romani vocabulary, but the original grammatical system is lost and replaced by the structure of the local language. This has happened massively in Spain, Scandinavia, the United Kingdom and occasionally elsewhere. These Para-Romani languages cannot be considered "Romani" any more, even though they are related to Romani in their vocabulary. They have become different languages, since they have very different grammatical structures. They cannot be considered the same language.

These people don't speak Romani: are they Gypsies?

There are also groups who are sometimes considered to be "Gypsies" who do not speak Romani, mostly in the Balkans. Some groups speak a form of Romanian (e.g. the Karavlax, Beash and Rudari groups), others Albanian (e.g. Ashkalije in Kosovo). There is a possibility that some of these groups were Roma who have lost their language. Some members of these groups claim a connection with the Roma, others deny this emphatically (this may also depend

ROMANIFOLKETS ORDBOK
Romani - Norsk - engelsk

Glimt fra en kristen Romanislekt i Norge - v. Ludvig Karlsen
Ole Bjørn Saltnes:Det reiser seg et folk
Tall og regning
Knut Sørsdal: Romanifolkets historie
Ludvig Karlsen: Forord til ordlisten
Setninger på Romani og norsk
Om Ludvig Karlsen

Historikk på Romani, norsk og engelsk

Ninna rakrar vorsnus Romani. Miro pasjar vorsnus honkar jikk marnus. Ninna rakrar drabriske gana, vorsnus avar kei to timmlan bars 1500. Butt gana pasjar vorsnus honkar, manus teli fon Østen. Butt pasjar Midtøsten. Duri drom kammar vorsnus manus jadd. Butt baroli bars kammar jadd, ninna honkar vorsnus kei. Ninna honkar butt andri vorsnus manus, stedd oppri. Ninna honkar savot andri sass timlan. Tikno manus sitto vorsnus, avar auri sikkar siro. Vorsnus kammar kji ninna honka leiano vagos. Ninna dokkar vorsrius avri vorsnus Romani rakripa. Butt honkar avri vorsnus kjavoar, ternoe savo kji, rigrar rakra Romani. Savot vorsnus kerar Ninna, Randrar teli vorsnus rakripa, hilprar sass vorsnus manus to sjunna. Sass gana andri helko timmlan, kammar dokka avri, siros rakripa. Ninna kerar vorsnus solus.

Nå snakker vi Romani. Jeg tror vi er et folk. Nå sier beleste folk at vi kom hit til landet år 1500. Mange mennesker tror vi er et folk som kommer fra Østen. Flere tror Midtøsten. Lang vei har vårt folk gått. Mange hundre år har gått. Nå er vi her. Nå har mange innen vårt folk stått opp. .Nå er det slik i alle land. Små folkeslag lik oss kommer ut og viser seg. Vi har ikke noe å være flaue over. Nå gir vi ut vårt Romanispråk. Mange av våre barn og unge, klarer ikke å snakke Romani. Slik vi gjør nå, skriver ned vårt språk, hjelper vi alle i vårt folk til å forstå sitt språk. Alle folk i hele verden har gitt ut sitt språk. Nå gjør også vi det.

Now we speak Romani. I believe we are a people. Scholars say that we came to this country about the year 1500. Many people believe we are a people group that came from the East. Many believe from the Middle East. A long way our people have travelled. Hundreds of years has passed. Now we are here. Now many of our people have stood up. Now there are so in many countries. Small people groups like us come out and show themselves. We have nothing to be ashamed of. Now we give out our Romani-language. Many of our children and our young people can not speak Romani. When we do this, writing down our language, we help people to understand their language. People all over the world have published their language. Now we do it too!

Norwegian Romani or Rommani is one of those rare varieties in which the lexicon is all Romani, but the word endings and structure of the sentence is from another language, here Norwegian. The same text is given in both Norwegian and English.

on the region), and it is, of course, up to themselves how these people define their identity. If they were ethnically Roma, some Romani words would survive in their speech but that is not the case. The Travellers of Ireland and the Abdal of Turkey and elsewhere do not share the same origin as the Roma. There may be contacts and connections but the groups consider themselves distinct, and this is confirmed by the fact that their languages have nothing in common with Romani.

The language situation in the United Kingdom

The Romanichal Gypsies in Britain speak a language they call Romanes (Rommanes), Romani or Pogadi Jib. However, the Romanichal can hardly understand the Romani speakers from Eastern Europe, even though many of their words are the same. This is because they combine the Romani vocabulary with their variety of English, as discussed above. Scholars have found a few dozen languages which ingeniously combine the vocabulary of one language with the endings, sounds and structure of another. Other scholars would regard this as impossible but the language of the Romanichals is the proof that it can be achieved.

The variety of Romani which was formerly spoken in Wales, but which now seems to have disappeared, would have been reasonably mutually intelligible with Romani from Eastern Europe. Both the "mixed" (Para-Romani) and "unmixed" varieties were already documented around 1600, and they seem to have co-existed for several centuries in the UK.

Apart from these groups that have lived in Britain for four hundred years, there are also more recent Romani-speaking immigrants in the United Kingdom, mainly from the Czech Republic, Romania and Poland. They speak the type of Romani which is the subject of this book.

The language situation in Ireland

In Ireland there are groups of people who live in caravans and travel from campsite to campsite. They are called "Gypsies" by many of the Irish, as their life style is similar to that in the popular image of Gypsies or Roma. These groups in Ireland like to call themselves "Travellers" when speaking English, and "Minceir" in their own language. They call their language "Gammon". The language of these Irish Travellers has no connection with the language of the Roma or British Romanichals, apart from a few words which each has borrowed.

The language of the Irish Travellers is not Romani. There are clear traces of Irish Gaelic in their language but much of it is of undetermined origin.

Diversity

To summarise, Roma may have had different reasons to shift to other languages but the number of speakers is still large enough so that it can be considered a healthy language.

Romani is a language with an undetermined number of dialects, comparable in range and variation with German or English. The different varieties of the language show influences from many European languages but under the cloak of recent influences, there is solid unity of the Romani language. Students of Romani dialects are continuously struck by their similarities, unique features and shared irregularities, in all the different areas where the language is spoken. On linguistic grounds it is therefore certain that the ancestors of the Roma were one group when they entered Europe.

Romani has also led to the creation of mixed languages, the existence of which has baffled linguists. There are linguists who claim that such languages cannot exist. The Para-Romani varieties show that they are wrong.

Romani words have furthermore entered several other forms of speech, such as that of some groups of Travellers and non-standard varieties of several languages.

VI. Romani in public life

Like all languages, Romani is first and foremost a way of communicating by talking. Many people nevertheless believe that "language" and "writing" are more or less the same thing, perhaps because this is how they are presented in schools. When you "do English", you read literature, write essays and work on punctuation and spelling.

Like many minority languages, the use of Romani has not generally been encouraged, and as a result the language has a relatively limited tradition of writing and other forms of public use. Romani is mostly spoken at home and in the Romani communities. It has not always been possible to use Romani in public or in the media. Nevertheless, there are numerous ways in which Romani is used in public. In this chapter we will discuss some of these, such as meetings, publications and different kinds of media, including theatre, television and the Internet, as well as the use of Romani in the educational system.

Suppression of the Romani language

Historically, Romani has generally been discouraged and often banned outright. This was already happening centuries ago in Hungary, Spain and a number of other countries. In Spain, anyone caught speaking Romani would have his or her tongue cut out. Maria Theresa in Hungary wanted to make the Roma undistinguishable from Hungarian citizens and banned their language. Her decrees of 1761 and 1767 ordered twenty-five lashes for those who spoke

P H E Ň A L E   P H R A L A L E   R O M A L E !

Ušten opre ! Uštavas jekh avres ! Avľa amaro dives, pre savo užaneras amare daja but berš. Oda dives imar adaj hino. P e r š i v a r o Roma, so dživen andre kadi phuv, šaj chuden peskeri bacht andre peskere vasta. Akana hin pre amende, sar pes dovakeraha, sar džanaha te likerel jekhetane, so keraha angle amare čhave.

Amenge kampel te likerel ajsedženenca, so kamen te šunel amaro lav, amaro čačipen. Oda hin OBČANSKÉ FORUM. O Občanské forum udzanľa amari romani sera.

Romská občanská iniciatíva

Občanské forum the Romani občansko iniciativazaačhen savore Romen andre amari phuv. Vazdas upre amaro romipen perdal o feder dživipen! Ma bisteras amare dadengero čačipen : PAŤIV DES, PAŤIV ARAKHES.

S E S T R Y   B R A T I A   R O M O V I A

Prebuďte sa! Prebúdzajme jeden druhého! Prišiel deň, na ktorý naši predkovia čakali dlhé roky. Ten deň je tu. Romovia, ktorý žijú v tejto krajine, možu po prví raz vziať svoj osud do vlastných rúk. A teraz je na nás, ako sa dohodneme, ako budeme držať spolu a čo urobíme pre svoje deti.

Spojme sa s ľudmi, ktorí sú ochotný počuť naše slovo a našu pravdu. Je to OBČIANSKÉ FÓRUM. Občianske fórum uznalo našu stranu.

Romská občianská iniciatíva

Občianské fórum a Romská občianská iniciatíva stojí za všetkými Romami v tejto krajine. Pozdvihnime svoje romstvo pre lepší život. Nezabúdajme na pravdu našich otcov : DAJ ÚCTU, DOSTANE SA TI ÚCTY.

Romská občianska iniciatíva

Zástupcovia Romskej občianskej iniciatívy Jan Rusenko a Emil Ščuka. Spojenie : Jan Rusenko, Husinecká 27, Praha 3 - Žižkov, 130 00

This pamphlet in Romani and Czech
was distributed during the velvet revolution in Czechoslovakia.

Romani. Prohibition of the language was only one step in a campaign to eliminate the Roma altogether. Being a Rom could in itself carry a death penalty. The consequences of these measures were manifold and loss of the language was certainly the least serious of these.

This banning of the Romani language was not limited to earlier centuries. Indeed, the suppression of the language has continued into the 20th century. In 1939 the Slovak state outlawed the Roma for speaking Romani. The anti-Gypsy policy of the Nazis and the attempted genocide of the Roma of course had destructive consequences for the Romani language too.

After the Second World War the suppression of the language continued. In some areas of the Czech Republic Romani children had to pay one crown for each Romani word that they used in class. The communist party of Czechoslovakia took a decision at their plenary meeting in April 1958 that "it would be reactionary to create a literary Gypsy language on the basis of scattered Gypsy dialects. It would conserve the Gypsy primitive way of life and isolate them from the working class". As recently as the 1980s it was forbidden to print Romani in Bulgaria.

Such restrictions happened not only in Eastern Europe. Germany, for example refused to acknowledge Romani as a minority language to be protected by the European Charter of Regional and Minority Languages arguing that it is not the language of a particular region. Sinti has been spoken on German territory continuously for some 500 years.

There are many more illustrations of how the Romani language and people have been persecuted and oppressed. These events had a deep impact on the Roma. Some groups have responded by clinging even more tenaciously to their language and customs, while others have lost part or all of their language, and others, notably the Sinti, do not want outsiders to learn their language, or even to know about it. Some may even deny that they have their own language but that is exceptional. The majority of the Romani people have preserved their language and use it for a variety of purposes, but most commonly at home.

Is Romani used in singing?

If there is one aspect of Gypsy culture which is well known to the outside world, it is music. There are many different styles, and music may be instrumental or vocal. Many professional Romani groups and choirs sing both in Romani and in the language of the region where they reside. When they

Gel'em, gel'em

1. Gel'em, gel'em lungone dromençar
maladil'em baxtale Rromencar
A Rromale! len kotar tumen aven
e caxrençar, bokhale čhavençar?

2. Sàsa vi man bari familia,
mudardǎs la i kali lègia.
Saren čhindǎs vi Rromen vi Rromněn
maškar lende vi cikne čhavorren.

3. Putar devl'a te kale udara
te šaj dikhav murri familia.
Palem ka žav lungone dromençar.
Ta ka phirav baxtale Rromençar.

4. Opre Rroma, isi vaxt akana
ajde mançar sa lumiaqe Rroma.
O kalo muj ta kale jakha
Kamàva len sar e kale drakha.

The song "Gelem, Gelem" can be considered the Romani national anthem.

play for non-Romani audiences, for instance at weddings, they are especially likely to sing in other languages. Among themselves, Romani is more often used.

There has been a long tradition of recording and producing Romani music on records and CDs. There are countless numbers of albums wholly or partly in Romani. Most well-stocked record stores have a "Gypsy music" section which will contain recordings in Romani as well. In a few cases the lyrics of the songs are included on the cover.

The song *Gelem, Gelem* (I went, I went) is sometimes considered the Romani hymn. It is often played at Roma meetings. It is based on a traditional song. This song was featured in Petrovic's film *I Even Met Some Happy Gypsies,* with a few lines added. The final two verses were composed by Jarko Jovanovic during the first World Romani Congress in 1971.

Is there theatre in Romani?

A theatre play of 1646 from Italy is one of the earliest sources of the Romani language – albeit it only a dozen lines. After that there is no documentation of the use of Romani on stage until the 20th century.

Roma have been depicted by non-Romani actors in the theatre for many centuries. These characters, however, do not use Romani, although in some cases they use a language other than the local one, showing that playwrights are aware that Roma have a language of their own. "Stage Gypsies" are often portrayed as speaking Rotwelsch (German "cant") or a trade language.

In Turkey there is an old tradition of shadow theatre called Karagöz. Although today the plays are exclusively in Turkish, Roma have played a role in the development and diffusion of this medium. Some of the puppets used clearly have a Romani origin, and some of the associated terms and names also come from Romani. Evliya Çelebi, the famous traveller-scholar from Turkey, witnessed Roma in Edirne (Turkey) performing shadow theatre as early as in 1650.

It was perhaps only in the 20th century that Roma became active in specifically Romani-language theatre in the former Soviet State. In 1931 the Romani theatre company *Romen* was established in Moscow, with Michael Jaščin as the first director. Their first production, *Žizn na kolesach* "Life on wheels", was written by the Rom writer Alexandr Germano. The actors were untrained, natural talents. The company still exists. The plays are mostly in Russian, with some dialogues and all the songs in Romani. The Romen theatre has had much influence on many generations of Romani singers, musicians, actors and dancers.

Some years after the Second World War a Slovak Romani woman called Ilona Lacková (born 1921) wrote a play called *Horiací Cigánsky tábor* "The Burning Romani colony". The play was mostly in Slovak, with some songs and dialogues in Romani. The theme was based on her own bitter experiences from the war when inhabitants of Romani settlements were expelled to remote locations. Lacková herself staged the play with her sisters, brothers-in-law and other Roma from their settlement. The play was a tremendous success: it was played 106 times between 1948 and 1950 in East Slovakia and the western Czech lands. Her life story was recorded in Romani by Milena Hübschmannová and after transcribing and translating it was published in Czech and earlier last year, in English.

Probably the most famous of all Romani theatre groups is the professional company *Teatro Roma Pralipe* ("brotherhood"). The actors and director are originally from Yugoslavia but they moved to Germany in the late 1980s. The group was founded in 1971 in Skopje (today the capital of the Republic of Macedonia). They now have their base in Mülheim an der Ruhr. Their director, Rahim Burhan, is also an inspiring leader. They perform mostly internationally famous dramas, especially translated into Romani by and for the group. Their plays include Shakespeare's *Romeo and Juliet*, Federico García Lorca's *Blood Wedding* and Sophocles' *King Oedipus*. They also attract audiences of non-Roma, who get a written summary of the play to help them follow it. They are successful with different audiences and they have won several prizes at festivals.

In 1984 a theatre company was founded by Emil Ščuka in Sokolov, North Czechoslovakia. Ščuka had studied half a year in Moscow and became inspired by the Moscow *Romen* company. He obtained a law degree and became a prosecutor in Sokolov. The first play, *Amaro Drom* "our way", written by Ščuka, was only partly in Romani, but the company's second play, a dramatised tale called *God'aver Rom the dilino Beng* "The clever God and crazy Devil", was entirely in Romani. The reaction of the Romani audience to the public use of Romani on stage was tremendous. The producer was embraced and elderly Roma broke out in tears. Sadly, the group closed down in 1989.

In 1994 the Slovak Romani journalist Anna Koptová founded a theatre group called *Romathan* in Košiče, East Slovakia. This group performs bilingual plays. They perform both their own work, such as their first performance *Tabor*

The Roma theatre group Romathan from Slovakia, which performs its plays in the Romani language.

Uchodit v Nebo / Cikáni jdou do nebe "Gypsies go to heaven", and translated work, such as Federico García Lorca's "Blood Wedding", with the title *Ratvale Bijava*. They also perform dramatised tales for children.

Are there films in Romani?

The Romani film industry is an emerging industry and so there are only a few films in the language but there are some feature films in the Romani language. Some of these were made by Roma, others were made by non-Roma. An early example is Alexander Petrovic's film *Skupljaci Perja* (the collectors of feathers), more widely known under the name *I Even Met Some Happy Gypsies*, which came out in the 1960s in Yugoslavia. Probably the most famous film in Romani is Emil Kusturica's film *Time of the Gypsies*, a long movie (all in Romani) about Yugoslavian Roma who move to Italy. It stimulated intense discussions among Roma and was a great success, both among Gypsies and non-Gypsies.

Filmmaker Tony Gatliff made several films in Romani, among them "Gadžo Dilo" and "Latcho Drom".

The best known Rom film maker is Tony Gatliff from France. His most famous films are *Les Princes* and *Latcho Drom* (literally "good road", or "good trip"). The first is in French and the second a music documentary in which Romani is also used. The latter has won several prizes and is appreciated both by Roma and non-Roma. Gatliff's film *Gadžo Dilo* "Crazy Stranger" is almost completely in Romani. Other Roma in the film industry are Tom Merino (USA) and Dodo Banyák (Slovakia), but Romani is not the main language used in their films.

There are, of course, hundreds of documentaries about Roma in which the Romani language is used. These are mostly made for television rather than cinemas. An example of a documentary film wholly or partially in Romani is *T'aves baxtalo* (Netherlands, 1994), a documentary about three groups of Romanian Roma.

There are also documentaries which were (co-)produced by Roma. An example is the film (mostly in Romani) *Amen sam so amen sam* ("We are who we are") which was a production of the Burgenland Roma Organisation *Verein Roma* in

Austria (1993, 1995), and the film *Gelem, Gelem* produced in Germany in 1992. The Sinti-Romani Melanie Spitta has co-operated with German film director Katrin Seibold on a number of documentaries in which Romani is often used as the language of interviews.

Is Romani used in official assemblies?

As far as is known, Romani has never been used in a national parliament. Even though a few countries have decided to make special provision for Romani as a minority language, it is not used in debates. Some countries, such as Hungary and Spain, had or have Roma in the parliament but these Roma use the state language.

There have been four world Romani congresses at which Romani was used. In international political and cultural meetings Romani is the language commonly used. Sometimes simultaneous interpretation is provided from Romani into other languages, or into Romani if the speaker does not use Romani. This has been the case at a number of conferences on Roma-related issues.

At scientific conferences Romani is hardly ever used, except occasionally at conferences relating to Roma and the Romani language. At the second conference on Romani linguistics in Amsterdam, for instance, three papers, those by Jorge Bernal, Marcel Cortiade and George Sarău, were presented in the Romani language. Other subjects, including medical ones, have occasionally been discussed in Romani at conferences.

Do governments use Romani?

Governments rarely use Romani for official publications. An exception is Macedonia, where it was one of the languages used in their 1994 census. The USA 2000 census forms are also available in Romani.

Are there translators/interpreters for Romani?

Almost all Roma know at least one other language besides Romani, and in legal cases they will usually have an interpreter for their second language, e.g. Albanian or Romanian in Germany. Some Roma insist, for good reasons, in having an interpreter for Romani rather than their second language.

In several countries there are interpreters for Romani, who interpret for instance for asylum procedures, refugee committees, court cases and in meetings between Roma and non-Roma. Both Roma and non-Roma do this kind of work. In court procedures Romani interpreters are used in a number of countries, such as the Czech Republic, Germany, Netherlands and the United Kingdom. In the last country, training courses culminating in a certificate for Romani translation are available.

Can Romani be written?

Any language can be written and Romany is no exception. Writing is a way of putting speech sounds into visual symbols so that speech can be transmitted without the use of sounds. It has to be stressed that spoken language is the basic form of communication. Writing is derived from spoken language. Oral language is much more common, more frequent and more basic than written communication.

There are different ways of converting sounds into visual forms. The alphabetic way – used in this book – is the most familiar to the reader, as all European languages make use of it. It is a way of writing in which, ideally, one sound is represented by one letter. Due to historical developments and changes in the languages, spelling is usually more complicated than that, especially in languages such as English which have a long written history.

As far as is known, Romani was written for the first time in the 16th century, when Andrew Borde wrote down a number of sentences from a Rom he met, probably at an inn in Calais or England. These were published in 1542. Writing in Romani remained rare until the 1800s. Before that time, there are only word lists from different areas, a few song texts, a theatre fragment and a few dialogues written down by curious travellers and the like.

The oldest text written in Romani by a Gypsy is probably the text of a letter from a Sinti man to his wife which was published in 1755 with a German translation (see following pages).

The Latin alphabet, used for western European languages, is not the only script used for writing Romani. In Greece, for instance, Romani is mostly written with the Greek alphabet (although very little seems to be written in Romani in Greece). In Russia and Serbia the Cyrillic (Russian) writing system is used. The Arabic script has also been used, for example, in Iran. More importantly, the first periodical produced by Roma for Roma was printed in the Arabic script in the 1920s in Edirne in Turkey. It was called *Laćo* which means "good".

Beytrag
zur Rotwellischen Grammatik,
Oder:
Wörter = Buch,
Von der
Zigeuner = Sprache,
Nebst einem
Schreiben
eines Zigeuners an seine Frau,
darinnen er ihr von seinem elenden Zustande,
in welchem er sich befindet, Nachricht
ertheilet.

Frankfurt und Leipzig, 1755.

Hoch-Deutsch.	In Zigeuner-Sprache.
# Brief.	# Liel.
## Meine liebe Frau!	## Mirikomli Romni!

Ich bin von Frankfurth nach Neustadt gereiset: Unterwegens habe viele Beschwerlichkeiten ausgestanden. Meine Mitgesellen zanckten sich immer; Es war kalt und schlimm Wetter; die Kinder wurden kranck; meine Herberge worinn ich eingekehret, brannte ab; meine Ziege und das jüngst gebohrne Kalb sind davon gelauffen; das Flachs, Hampf und die Wol-

Ertiwlum Francfurt tatterwium Tegaijum apro Newoforo: aprodrum nelis mange mishdo, mare manush tshingerwenes Ketteni, Tshiel niste midshach Wettra; Tshawewle nas wele dowa Keer, kaime gaijam medre gazdias Tele, mare ziga Toterno Kalbo nählsle penge, o Flachso, Te Hanfa, Te Wul-

Hoch-Deutsch.	In Zigeuner-Sprache.

le, so meine Schwiegerin und Stief-Tochter gesponnen, sind verbrant. Kurz: ich war so arm, daß wir fast alle nackend waren. Ich dachte mich durch Holtzhauen und meiner Hände Arbeit, oder durch Handel und Wandel zu nähren; alleine keiner wollte von mir etwas kauffen, oder etwas zum Pfande annehmen, ich wurde vielmehr von einer Bande Soldaten überfallen, welche viele von uns verwundet, drey getödtet, und mich auf ewig auf eine Festung gebracht. Der Himmel bewahre dich,

la, Te Shwigarizakri, Te Stiff Tshakri ho spin derde gatshias nina Lopennawawa wium Ketshorero Tewiam Hallauter nange. Denkerdum Tshinger wammangi kasht, Temre was Tiengri butin, oder hunte di kaw Te Kinnaw Tschommoni, pre, Te bikkewaw pale, Te de denkerwaw Te ernährwaw mann Kiacke mebium Kiake Kuremangrender pene a permande, buten Tshinger de, buten, thri nen marde, Timman Tshimaster apri butin tshidde obollo ben

-❧ (o) ❧-   **89**

Hoch-Deutsch.   **In Zigeuner-Sprache.**

Dich vor einem sol-   Terackel Tutt an-
chen Unglück, und   dre fawe kolefter
ich beharre   kaime wiumadre,
Te me tshawa Ti-
rerum

Dein getreuer   Shinandro
Mann.   Meraben.

*This letter that a Sinti man had sent to his wife is one of the first pub-
lished texts of a Romani speaking person. It was published in 1755 in
Germany, with a German translation. the first lines mean: "My dear wife,
I travelled from Frankfurt to Neustadt (the word used in Sinti is the liter-
al translation of the name of this town 'New City').
On my way I had to endure many difficulties ..."*

All these ways of writing are also (more or less) alphabetic, and any language, can be written in any alphabetical script.

There are also Roma who have devised their own writing system, such as those living in Bulgaria, the Czech Republic, Finland, Latvia and Russia.

Until the 20th century, most writing in Romani was done by non-Gypsies. This is partly because the language is used mostly for talking and partly because many Roma could not read or write. Those Roma who could read and write had learned to do so in a language other than Romani and therefore preferred to carry on writing in the other language. Nevertheless, there is a growing body of literature in Romani. More and more is being written and published in Romani, by and for Roma.

Is Romani used in poetry?

Like all human beings, Roma have feelings and expressive needs, and so Roma write poetry, sometimes in Romani but also in other languages. Numerous poetry anthologies have been published, often bilingual, in Romani with translations into another language. Poets who have produced several poetry books in Romani include Papusza from Poland, Santino Spinelli from Italy, Leksa Manuš from Latvia, Károly Bari from Hungary, N. Pankov, A. Germano, N. Satkievich from Russia, Jan Horváth, Vlado Oláh, Margita Reiznerová from Slovakia, Tera Fabiánová from the Czech Republic, Luminitsa Cioaba from Romania and Rajko Djurić from Yugoslavia/Germany. There are also many poems published in periodicals produced by Roma.

Every year the Romani organisation *Them Romano* ("Romani land") in Italy organises international Romani poetry contests. This has led to a number of publications and anthologies of poetry in Romani. There have been similar competitions in the Czech Republic, with hundreds of competitors.

Occasionally poems have been written in Romani by non-Roma, such as the English librarian/linguist John Sampson. He also wrote a comprehensive grammar of Romani as spoken in Wales. He published a Romani poetry book *Romane Gilja* and wrote numerous published and unpublished poems as well as letters in Romani.

The preceding paragraphs discussed written poems. Much poetry is also oral. Song texts, for instance, can be seen as a form of poetry. This is especially true for some of the improvised songs. Among the Lovari there are excellent

This woman, Nada Braidic, won the first price in a Romani poetry contest organised by Them Romano in Italy, in 1994.

improvised poems ("slow songs") which are sung to more or less established melody lines. These often relate to recent highlights and important events in the Roma community.

Is there literature (fiction) in Romani?

Romani writers have been able to form a modest Romani division of the international association of writers, the PEN Club. There are also Romani authors in the International Pen Club, such as Valdemar Kalinin, not all of them write in Romani. For instance, Matéo Maximoff, a Russian-French Rom, who died in 1999, wrote some of his books in French rather in his native Romani. He has also written in Romani which he later translated into French.

In the former Soviet Union there was a privileged and élite Union of Poets and Writers with strict requirements for admission. A number of Roma were admitted as members: Alexander Germano (1893-1954), Nikolai Pankov (1895-1956), Ivan Rom-Lebedev (1901-89), Nikolai Satkievich (1917-91), Ivano Romano (Pantchenko) (born 1941) and Valdemar Kalinin (born 1946).

Literature in the Romani language is only now emerging. For most publishers books in Romani are not economically viable, because of the difficulty of international distribution to the potential readers in widely scattered Roma communities. Until recently, most publications in Romani were therefore aimed at an audience with an academic interest. These were studies by and for linguists, folklorists and the like, who had an interest in Gypsy culture. Many of these publications were transcripts of recorded oral stories. Roma as well as non-Roma were active in collecting and publishing these stories.

"O Rukun ʒal and-i skòla" is one of a few dozen books for children that were produced in Romani. It has been translated from the English book "Spot goes to School".

This has changed only recently. In former Yugoslavia and the Czech Republic in particular, original novels, biographies and storybooks for children, aimed at other Roma rather than academics were produced in Romani. These publications have had an important impact in the Roma communities.

Some works of world literature have been translated into Romani as well, obviously for a Romani audience. Some of Pushkin's work for instance, was translated from Russian as early as the 1930s and so were some of Shakespeare's dramas and Tolstoy's prose. A few children's books, such as Saint-Exupéry's *Le Petit Prince* ("The Little Prince") also exist in a Romani translation. Some of the illustrated "Spot" books were published in a standardised form of Romani. One Indian epic work has been published in a Romani translation, as has the poetry of Omar Khayyam.

Roma culture is mainly an oral culture, however. In many countries there are people who are especially esteemed as storytellers. Some have a huge repertoire of fairy tales, tall tales and epic stories. Typically, the listeners comment on these stories afterwards, sometimes claiming that some detail (e.g. the number of princesses present at a feast) was not correct.

Oral literature is much more important for most Roma than written literature. Many Roma may not even be aware of the existence of written literature in their own language. Some may even state that it cannot be written but this is disproved by the existence of dozens of books in Romani.

Is there a Romani Bible translation?

The oldest printed Bible translation in a Gypsy language is the translation of the Gospel of Luke into Caló. This translation was published in 1837. Caló as spoken in Spain is derived from Romani but it does not have the same grammatical system as Romani. That has been replaced by the grammatical system of Spanish (a so-called Para-Romani variety, see Chapter V).

There are countless other Bible translations which have been printed and distributed in many different dialects. There are, for instance, translations of the Acts of the Apostles into Czech Romani (1936); translations of the Gospel John into Lettish Romani (1933), into Sinti (1930), Finnish Romani (1971) and Slovak Romani (1997); the Gospel of Mark into Sinti (1912 and 1994) and the Gospel Matthew into Lovari in Hungary (1991) and into Baltic Romani (1995 and 1999). There are also adaptations of Bible stories in several varieties, including Sinti, Slovak Romani and the language spoken by English Gypsies.

A number of complete Romani New Testaments are available such as the one by the Alliance Biblique in the Kalderash dialect in 1990, and another – Balkan Romani – version published by the Adventist Press in Sofia in 1995.

Some Old Testament fragments have been published and complete translations are in preparation. The Jewish religion has hardly any adherents among the Roma.

The oral orientation of the Roma plays a role in their religious life, too. There are cassettes of religious texts and songs which circulate among Roma from all over the world, in particular those who belong to the Pentecostal church.

Are there Romani translations of other religious books?

Romani translations of the Koran exist but, as far as is known, none have been published. Many Roma in the Balkans and Turkey are Muslims, and several use the Romani language in their religious services. Some Roma communities have handwritten versions of the Koran in Romani.

The Rāmāyanam, an ancient epic work from India, was published in Baltic Romani in India by Roma Publications. Some Roma feel a connection with India since their language came from there. The number of Hindus among Roma is negligible, however.

Are there other books in Romani?

There are some practical texts in Romani. In the former Soviet Union brochures and booklets were produced in Romani between 1925 and 1938 on subjects such as how to mend a tractor, how to grow crops, how to study, etc. There were several hundred titles, all in Cyrillic script.

There are other non-fiction books in Romani published outside the Soviet Union, but not as many as in comparable languages with millions of speakers. There is a book about the sad fate of the Sinti and Roma in the Second World War, a grammar book of the Romani language and a course in Sranan Creole (a language of Surinam in South America). There is a biography of Tito and a book on people who received military decorations in what was then Yugoslavia. The periodicals Romano Džaniben, Studii Romani and others contain many informative texts in Romani as well. Other periodicals produced by Roma in many countries also contain essays and articles in Romani.

Are there periodicals in Romani?

Most Roma who learn to read and write do so in the language that they learned in school – and that is seldom Romani. For that reason most of the periodicals that Roma produce are not in Romani but in an official local language (e.g. Czech, English, German, Serbian). Some papers may have a Romani title, or occasional articles in Romani, but most of the content is in a second language. There are, or have been, a number of bilingual periodicals, such as *Patrin* (international, Romani and English), *Romano Centro* from Vienna (German and Romani), *Romano Patrin* in Austria (Romani and German) and *Rom Po Drom* (Polish and Romani). Most of these cover regional and international news concerning Roma.

There are even a few periodicals for children in Romani, such as *Miri Tikni Mini Multi* from Austria, *Luludi* from Slovakia, *Kereka* from the Czech Republic and *Čhavrikano Lil* from Serbia. As mentioned above, there have been periodicals in Romani from at least the early decades of this century. The oldest one known dates from the 1920s.

Is Romani taught in schools?

In 1925 the former Soviet Union recognised Romani as one of the languages of national minorities. In the following period Romani was introduced in schools and the first Romani textbooks were published in the Xaladytko (North Russian) dialect. At the same time over 300 Romani books for adults were published. This ended by 1939.

After 1945, the Communist governments which were established in Central and Eastern Europe, were sometimes positively disposed towards minorities, including the Roma. This was more so in Hungary and Yugoslavia than in Bulgaria and Czechoslovakia, where there was a strong pressure towards assimilation. Government policy was mostly aimed at providing education to all citizens, including the Roma, in the official languages. There were no cases where Roma pupils received instruction in or about their own language.

From the 1970s onwards schools in some Western European countries (Finland, France, Germany and Sweden) started to use Romani in special education programmes for Romani children. This resulted in a number of ABC books and textbooks for schools. Some popular children's books were also translated into Romani, for example, some of the work of Astrid Lindgren was translated

Romani speaking children in school.

into Kalderash. This is a continuing process and the number of schools using Romani is increasing, for instance in Austria and Germany.

In Eastern Europe, especially after the democratic changes of 1990, Romani has gradually been taking its place in the schools. Romani textbooks and ABC-books have been published in many countries, such as Bulgaria, the Czech Republic, Hungary, Latvia, Macedonia, Romania, Russia, Slovakia and former Yugoslavia. There have been several training courses for the teaching of Romani intended for Romani speakers.

In Hamburg (Germany), the Board of Education has been employing Romani teachers as assistant teachers since 1992. Their task is to support Romani children at school, as well as to provide native language instruction several hours a week. There are special Romani speaking teaching assistants to help with educational problems of Roma children, in the Czech Republic and Slovakia. In Košiče (East Slovakia) there is a high school for Roma musicians, dancers and actors where Romani is a compulsory subject.

There are also a number of special schools for Roma, where classes are taught in and about the Romani language. In Hungary there are the Gandhi school in Pecs and the Kalyi Yag school. This activity remains somewhat marginal.

A school for the performing arts in Slovakia uses Romani as a language of instruction. Romani is also used as a language of instruction in Moscow by Lev Cherenkov, in the Teachers Training College *Ny* and also in secondary schools where there are Romani classes. It is the working language of the private school *Studio Luludi* ("Flower") run by Ganga Batalova and Dr. Nadia Belugina. There is also a junior school in Ventspils (Latvia) where Romani is a working language.

Education of Romani children remains a special topic of attention. Regular international conferences have been organised to discuss the questions and problems of the education of Roma children in mainstream schools and in special Roma classrooms. Parents may consider schools as a threat to the preservation of their culture. Some forms of behaviour in school situations may be shocking to Roma parents as they contradict their strict ideas of hygiene or their traditions of politeness. Many parents are aware of this and in 1998 Sinti in the Netherlands and Germany made a video about school, mainly for parents of Romani-speaking children.

Similarly, after 1995 special learning aids, a video, and an animated film in Romani for children of the Romani asylum seekers from Eastern Europe were produced in London.

The European Charter for Minority Languages makes no special arrangements for the teaching of Romani, much to the distress of some Romani organisations. A recommendation by the Council of Europe from 1992 calls for the establishment of Romani study programmes.

Is Romani taught or studied at universities?

The Romani language is a subject of research for scholars in several fields. It is also taught, from a theoretical or structural point of view, in linguistics courses, and also in courses aimed at the acquisition of the language. Some of these courses are given by Roma with a university degree, for instance, in linguistics, and some are given by non-Roma. In the 1990s Romani was taught at universities in Austria (Graz, Innsbruck, Vienna), Bulgaria (Sofia), Czech Republic (Prague), Denmark (Aarhus), England (London, Manchester), France (Paris), Germany (Hamburg, Bochum), the Netherlands (Amsterdam), Romania

(Bucharest), Slovakia (Nitra, Ustí Nad Labem), the United States (Austin, Chicago, Pittsburgh) and probably elsewhere.

In Nitra (Slovakia) there is a whole department devoted to Romani studies and the Charles University in Prague offers a degree in *Studia Romistica* after five years of the study of the language, culture, history and folklore of the Roma. Some of the active scholars in the study of the language are themselves Roma: Ian Hancock of Austin, Texas, Hristo Kyuchukov of Bulgaria and Vania de Gila Kochanowski of Latvia and Paris.

Is Romani used on television and radio?

Songs in Romani can be heard occasionally on radio stations throughout Europe. There are also radio programmes in Romani in many places. In Vienna there are monthly programmes sponsored by the Romano Centro in which both Romani and German are used. In Paris there is a popular weekly programme, and also in other places there were or are radio programmes organised by

The weekly radio programme of the association "Romano Lil", Paris.

Roma. This is especially well developed in former Yugoslavia where there are or have been Romani-language radio stations such as Radio Prizreno in Kosovo and Romano Them in Belgrade (Serbia). In the Czech Republic there are Romani radio stations and also in Tvier (Russia) and Odessa (Ukraine). A 15-minute gospel programme in Romani is broadcast throughout the Balkans and Central Europe between 19.45 and 20.00 on Monday and Thursday (Medium wave 1395 kHz, wave length 215).

Romani can also be heard on the television, for example, when the documentaries and feature films discussed above are shown. In some countries, however, all films are dubbed in the official language so that Romani is not heard when such films are shown on television or in the cinema. Television programmes in Romani for Roma are relatively rare but they do exist, for example the weekly programme *Romale* in Prague. There are Romani television programmes in several places in former Yugoslavia, such as Belgrade in Serbia and Skopje in Macedonia. Usually they broadcast only a few hours a month.

Is Romani used on the Internet?

Romani is not only used for oral and written communication but also for electronic communication. There is a chatline for Roma on the Internet in which Romani is used. This is called *Drakhin*, the Romani word for a "grapevine", which by extension is used for a "network" in Romani. There is also Patrin (which superseded Romnet), which is open to both Roma and non-Roma and

```
Date sent:     Thu, 12 Nov 1998 20:32:11 -0500 (EST)
To:            romnet-l@smtp.teleport.com
Subject:       Re: [Romnet] RE. Monica
Send reply to: romnet-l@lists.teleport.com

Te aven baxtale !
Sosko Rom vaj Romni mangel/kamel e kerel mansa kommunikazija ande Romani
chip ?

Marko D.
==========================================

Me som chajori, 16 bershend, me mangav te rakirav tusa. Bi perasango,
O drago Del andas tut mor'e. Baxt, tai sastchipe, tuke tai che niamoske.

Devlesa,

O Dufunia
```

An example of an email in Romani. This questions means: Which Romani man or woman wants to communicate with me in Romani? And the answer begins with: I am a girl, 16 years old, I want to talk you.

Patrin

The Patrin Web Journal:
Romani Culture and History

Welcome to Patrin, dedicated to Romani (Gypsy) culture and history and to extending awareness of the continuous Roma struggle to achieve and maintain dignity and freedom. Patrin is a learning resource and information centre about Romani culture, social issues, and current events. To Roma the world over, we send the message: we will remember!

Románe! Phralále! Patrin si katé ando Internet te phenél le gadjénge pe amarí kultúra. Von kam primisarén amén máshkar lénde maj lashés te zhanén vórta kon sam thaj sar si amaró trájo. Atúnchi amé musáj te das vórba le gadjéntsa pe aménde aj kadiá amaró gláso kam avél ashundó. Amé trobúl te sam maj pachivalé le gadjéndar aj te arakhás amé pe mishtimáste. Kadeá amé shaj avás maj zuralé. Ashén Devlésa! But baxt aj sastimós tuménge!

Rom! Prale! Patrin hi-lo káte an u Internet te penél ap u gádje pre i mári kultúra. Jon dikén-le ap ménde fédar te djanéna mishtó kun ham unt har hi-lo maró djibén. Mu te rakrá mit u gádje pre ménde unt kjáke marí shtíma vel-li shundí. Mu te va érligedar unt kamlédar fun u gádje. An kajá shíkta amé va zorelédar. Chéna mit u Báro Dével! But baxt unt sastibén tuménge!

This is the homepage of Patrin on the Internet, which disseminates information about Roma. The introductory text is written in English, and in the Vlax and Sinti dialects of Romani.

has many hundreds of subscribers. The language most commonly used is English, but Romani is also frequently used and occasionally other languages such as French, Hungarian and Spanish. There are subscribers in all continents. Romanonet is a similar discussion list initiated in 1998.

Apart from these, there are a number of websites which provide information on the Romani language or which use the language. The website of the religious movement *Gypsies International* uses both English and Romani. The American Romani Union uses Romani sporadically and the Union Romaní in Spain uses English, Spanish and Romani. Websites which use the Romani language are listed on pp. 133-135 but the Internet changes quickly and some of the addresses may be outdated. Several websites list transcribed oral texts such as the website of the Romani programme in Graz (Austria).

VII. The future of the Romani language / Romani in the modern world

In this chapter we discuss some aspects of Romani in the modern world. We deal with its chances of survival, the development of the vocabulary and the development of a standard language.

Is Romani an endangered language?

Romani is listed in the UNESCO *Atlas of the World's Languages in Danger of Disappearing*, (Paris: UNESCO Publishing/ Canberra: Pacific Linguistics) as one of the languages in Europe which is endangered. It is certainly true that the language is on the retreat in several regions, and it is also true that a number of dialects are extinct or close to extinction. On the whole, however, there is no reason to fear the disappearance of Romani in the near future. The fact that the language has been preserved as a minority language for some 700 years in Europe shows the tenacity and the positive attitude of its speakers towards the language. This, despite the fact that the language has been repeatedly prohibited in various regions and that its speakers are subject to discrimination at all times almost everywhere.

On the other hand, pressure towards assimilation is greater than ever. Speakers of Romani are increasingly in contact with speakers of other languages. The impact of radio and television, the school system, the need for jobs and lack of official support, have also led to a shift towards other languages. This tendency is also visible in other European minority languages such as Welsh and Irish.

The number of speakers of Romani is hard to estimate but it is certainly over five million world wide, most of them living in Central and Eastern Europe (see Table 5 in Chapter III on p. 40). In many communities the language is spoken by all generations, and is transmitted normally to the children. Nevertheless, in some areas Romani is losing ground to other languages. We have already mentioned Bulgaria, Hungary and Turkey.

Some Romani dialects have died out or have only a few speakers left. Almost all of the speakers of the Havati dialect of Croatia, of the Czech Romani dialect and the Laiuse dialect of Estonia were massacred by the Nazis. Other dialects have disappeared because of action from governments who prohibited the speaking of Romani. This was the case for instance in Portugal, Spain and to some extent in Hungary, where the use of the language was forbidden centuries ago. More recently, pressure from other languages also plays a part, for instance in the school system, which has made Roma shift to other languages in recent times. Roma themselves may feel that by shifting to the language of the country they live in, they may gain better access to jobs.

But even in Romani communities where the language is being lost, there is a noticeable trend for young people to relearn the language that their parents or grandparents had preferred not to transmit to their children. This is especially the case when Roma shifted to another language, but still retained their ethnicity. We can also mention the phenomenon of Romani politicians whose family had lost the language, but who learned Romani to be able to communicate more directly with the Roma and to better represent them.

Dialect awareness

Easier travel possibilities and increased international awareness among Roma have expanded the knowledge among Roma of dialect differences. Some Roma intellectuals have felt a need for a unified, general form of Romani. But which form should it be?

Which dialect is used as a standard?

When states where different dialects of the national language are spoken, devise a standard language, two strategies are used. The "compromise" strategy combines those words and features that appear most often in the different dialects. This is, for instance, what happened in Norway with Nynorsk, and in the Netherlands. The other main approach is to encourage all speakers to adopt a single existing dialect, usually the one used in the centre of power, or the one used in an important religious work or an important city or region. This is what happened in France (the dialect of Paris), Spain (that of Madrid) and in the Arab world (that of the Koran). In many cases this is a natural process rather than a conscious choice.

These issues are more complicated for Romani speakers, partly because they are so widely scattered, partly because their different dialects have not all been written down and partly because no group or area is dominant. The fact is that many Roma are so poor that daily food for their children is much more important than the writing of their language and this plays a role. This means that no dialect of Romani is used as a standard.

Nevertheless, at international meetings of Romani speakers, Vlax dialects dominate to some extent, largely because these are spoken in most countries. Vlax Roma are the descendants of Romani slaves who left Romania after (and sometimes before) the abolition of slavery in Romania. When these people were set free, they spread all over Europe and beyond. While Vlax Roma may not be the largest Romani speaking group in a given country, speakers of other varieties are often to some extent familiar with Vlax dialects. Roma who attend international meetings are particularly aware of which words of their dialect are different in other dialects. They quickly learn to understand the equivalents in other dialects. They tend to avoid expressions which they know are particular to their own dialects. The main difficulty is posed by the presence of loanwords for many aspects of modern society borrowed from the various languages of the countries where different Roma live.

Jan Kochanowski bases his proposals of standardisation on his own dialect, the Baltic-Latvian. There has even been a proposal to introduce the Devanagari script (the script used for Indian languages) for Romani, but this has never been put into practice.

There have also been several proposals for creating a compromise standard language. Vlax dialects which are used at meetings are also used in some printed works. There is, for instance, a *Handbook of Vlax Romani* written by

Ian Hancock, published in the USA. In the USA, Vlax seems to be the only variety of Romani used in print, even though there are also quite a few speakers of other dialects. In Macedonia the locally dominant Arli dialect is used in most written work.

Is there a standard Romani language?

Romani has always been primarily an oral language. If people wrote it they often used an improvised way of spelling, based on the spelling of another language with which they were familiar. In more recent decades, with increasing international political and cultural contacts between Roma who speak different dialects, the need for a common Romani language is being felt among Romani intellectuals.

Every language in the world is spoken in different ways by different people in different places. For example, Londoners use some words that people in York do not, and vice versa. Also, they pronounce words differently. Neither is "more correct" than the other, but to communicate with each other, they need to agree what words and what pronunciation to use. They must share a set of words, grammatical rules and language norms. If there is none, speakers can resort to a process called "standardisation". Standardisation involves both the way words are written, i.e. the adaption of sounds to a writing system, and the vocabulary of a language.

For most languages, standardisation took a long time. Different choices were made for what the standard should be. In some countries (for example England)

	خ	
iß!	xā	خا
Reis	xābe	خاب
Nachricht	xābār	خابار
Höhle	xār	خار
Schwert *(Ġešlaġ , "Dorf der Goldschmiede")*	xārno	خارنو
in Ġučan und Mašhad	xānro	خاونر
Husten	xāsā	خاسا
Suppe, Reissuppe	xāšow	خاشو

Romani has been written occasionally in Arabic script. This is an example of a part of a word list from Roma in Iran. The first journal produced by Roma was also printed in Arabic script in the 1920's, before Turkey shifted to the use of the western, Roman alphabet.

the dialect of the centre of power was chosen to be the standard, and elsewhere the language of some important religious work (as in the Arabic countries) became the norm. Other countries developed an intermediate language created from different regional dialects. For Romani, only this last strategy could be an option.

To write a language which has not been written before, the use of an existing alphabet rather than creating a new one, is the obvious choice. Four alphabets are used in the area where Roma live: Roman or Latin (most of Europe), Cyrillic (e.g. Bulgaria, Russia, Serbia), Greek (Greece) and Arabic (Iran). The system most often used for Romani is the Latin script, and as most Roma also live in countries where the Roman alphabet is used that may be the best choice.

To use an existing alphabet, it has to be adapted for other languages, including Romani. The Latin alphabet has fewer letters than there are different speech sounds in most modern languages in Europe. Therefore, to distinguish all the distinct sounds of the Romani language the Latin alphabet must be modified. For English, for instance, letters like <k> and <x> were added. The same is true for the Cyrillic (Russian) alphabet, which has a few more letters than the Latin alphabet, but still not enough for a language like Romani.

For the use of the Latin alphabet, there are three main possibilities. The creation of new letters, or special signs beside or on top of letters, or several letters to symbolise one sound. Icelandic, for instance, uses some additional letters such

की
वृ ऋ रृ
ओदाकै
बूत् बेर्षंडी
दुब्देंस् मो ट्रोम् अकै
था अकना
सल प्रे मन्दी
पस्के ब्रिषिन्देस्केयंते

Romani has been written in one or two occasions in the Devanagari script of India.

as ð, whereas French uses accents, as in é and è, and so does Czech, as in č and ň. English uses double letters, as in 'ch' and 'sh', both of which symbolise just one sound. For Romani, several of these possibilities have been used in various forms of standardised writing.

In some countries, regional standard spellings of Romani have been developed. These standards are usually based on the dominant language of the region, to facilitate reading of the language. For instance, much of what is being printed in the Czech Republic uses more or less the same writing system as that used for the Czech language. Similarly, the Burgenland Roma of Austria opted for a spelling based on German for their dialect, without any accents or special signs. They use combinations of letters to indicate a different sound. In their spelling <ch> means the sound 'ch' as in Scottish "loch" or German "Bach" and <tsch> symbolises the same sound as in German "Tschüss" or English "church".

Most writing systems of Romani use the combinations <ph>, <kh> and <th> for certain consonants pronounced with a puff of breath (see p. 12 for some examples). In several countries, Romani is written in the Latin alphabet with the addition of accents added to letters to distinguish between sounds that the Latin alphabet does not cover.

In some areas such as Macedonia even a regional standard had an international orientation. The publication of a Romani grammar in Macedonian and Romani set the example for further writing. In 1992 there was a conference on the standardisation of the Romani language in Macedonia, sponsored by the board of education of the Republic of Macedonia. Both the grammar book and the standardisation conference were very influential in Macedonia. The standard was intended for Macedonia only. The fact that the conference chose the Roman alphabet rather than Cyrillic, indicates an international orientation.

At the World Romani Congress in Warsaw in 1990 it was decided to adopt as standard a Romani alphabet devised by Marcel Courtiade. This makes use of accents as well as new letters, such as θ. This is a letter in the Greek and Icelandic alphabet, but not in others. In the Romani writing system it sounds like /d/ or /t/. This standard alphabet has since been used for children's books, periodicals, school books, linguistic studies and several other publications, both of regional and international nature. Nevertheless, only a minority of what is being published in Romani uses this alphabet. It is not only a standardised way of writing but also a step in a proposal for a standard language. The people involved in this project also focus on the vocabulary and have already produced illustrated vocabulary books and a dictionary. A Romani encyclopaedia which draws on this concept is also in preparation.

An innovative project from Germany, where Romani immigrants from many countries came together, deserves mention here. A series of illustrated children's books *Jekh, Duj, Trin...* (one, two, three in Romani) carries text not in one standard language but in three different dialects of Romani side by side, in the same system of writing which includes accents or diacritics. This both symbolises the diversity of Romani, and also familiarises Romani children with slightly different varieties of their language thus stimulating an awareness and appreciation of those as well (see pp. 114-115).

Thus far we have been speaking about the written language but the spoken language is also undergoing a degree of standardisation. For instance, Romani members of the Pentecostal church send spoken religious tapes to fellow members in other countries who in this way become familiar with other dialects of Romani. It cannot be said yet that people will adopt items from the tapes, but practices like these increase knowledge of other dialects.

Romani vocabulary

Words for new things are often adopted at the same time as speakers first encounter them. For example the word "telephone", created from two Greek words, is used in dozens of European languages. Romani speakers also do this, but because they live in so many different countries, the languages from which they take over new words are varied. Technical, administrative and professional terms in particular differ from dialect to dialect and make international communication between Romani speakers difficult.

New words, extension of vocabulary

The shared vocabulary of the varieties of Romani is probably not sufficient to make communication about all subjects easy between speakers of different dialects. Several attempts have therefore been made to expand the vocabulary of Romani, both at a local level and even as an international standard. This task is, of course, especially urgent in the context of international communication.

As we mentioned above, many languages adopted the Greek word "telephone" when their speakers adopted this technology. Other languages, however, made up words of their own. For example German "Fernsprächgerät", literally "distant-talk-apparatus". Some people feel that Romani should use this method, coining new vocabulary on the basis of the existing Romani words. For instance,

1 • Who is smaller?

2 • It is straight.
The line is curved.
Is it straight or
curved?

3 • All have the
same length.
I dont't believe so.
How long are they.

7 • Now I am up.

8 / 9 • I see a
vase.
I see two faces.
What does the pic-
ture show?

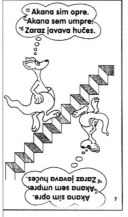

14 • Are the lines
bent?
This is an optical il-
lusion.

15 • Where is the
picture.
On the next page.

4 / 5 • Who speaks the truth?
Seven circles have the same size.
Eight circles have the same size.
Two circles have the same size.

6 • Place a German mark (coin) on the circle.
Is that a circle?
Maybe you can try.

10 • Do you paint a tree?

11 • No, a duck.
Where is the duck?

12 • I see twenty horses.
How many?
Count them!

Hold this page towards the sunlights.

No! It is true!

A series of booklets for children produced in Hamburg shows the same text in three different Romani dialects, one from Poland and two from former Yugoslavia.

instead of borrowing a word for "doctor", the Romani word for "medicine" can be used to create a word like "medicine man". Romani's grammatical system makes this possible. This strategy of expanding existing vocabulary has been used both spontaneously and in language planning.

A second strategy that has been used is the introduction of borrowings from Sanskrit (the parent language of Romani) or Hindi (one of Romani's sister languages in India). The Latvian-French linguist Jan Kochanowski, himself a native speaker of Romani, has made use of this strategy in his writings. A descriptive grammar of Romani written in Romani (produced in Macedonia in 1980) also used Hindi as a source of new words.

Another strategy has been to employ as many international terms as possible. In this system the word "international" would be expressed as *internacionalno*. It is felt that this would be easily understood and it makes use of the borrowing patterns of the Romani language. Supporters of the "Romani roots" strategy discussed above would prefer a word like *maškarthemutno*, literally "between-countries".

Strategies for preservation

We have discussed some ways in which Roma try to expand their language and make it internationally usable. Other strategies of preservation and expansion would be to increase the use of Romani in the primary education system, and to use it increasingly at meetings. The production of more publications in the language and its use in more types of media would also be important. A number of decisions by European governmental bodies provide the means of support for such activities.

Language and the economic situation

Many Romani children drop out of the education system too early, usually because there is no room in the system for their own cultural needs. It is important to keep in mind that language is only one not very important part of their culture.

This book deals with the language of the Roma. For most Roma, there are other things which are much more important than their language. As part of their culture, the language is transmitted to the next generation. But many Roma have problems much more serious than the preservation of the language. Many

Many Roma are so poor, that obtaining their daily food is much more important than writing their language.

live in poverty and suffer discrimination by both authorities and civilians. In some areas skinheads physically molest Roma and regularly kill them. These economic and social problems, however, are not directly connected to their language.

Outlook

Romani is a normal language with a fascinating history and one which has survived almost a millennium outside its area of origin, despite the oppression it has faced. It has been the subject of many scholarly studies, and it is used by a growing number of people in writing, films, media, poetry and on the Internet. It may be the only European language which is traditionally spoken as a native tongue in all Western and Eastern European countries.

The standardisation of Romani is only in its initial stages, and it is not yet certain what direction it will take. The fact that the Roma are so widely dispersed certainly complicates the task.

At any rate, Romani will continue to be spoken by many people but it is not clear to what extent the use of Romani will expand as a written language, or in what form or forms.

VIII. Scientific research on Romani

In this chapter we discuss some of the highlights of research on Romani, and some of the subjects that are studied today relating to the language.

The earliest documentation of Romani

The earliest research on Romani can be associated with the production of Romani word lists in the sixteenth century. In 1542 Andrew Borde published a short sample of Romani in his *Fyrst Boke of the Introduction of Knowledge*, and the first Romani vocabulary was published by Bonaventura Vulcanius in 1597. An Italian theatre play from 1646 contains some dialogues in Romani; in 1668 the Ottoman writer Evliya Çelebi presented samples of a Balkan Romani dialect, and Job Ludolf followed in 1691 with a German Romani word list. Numerous additional word lists appeared in print in the first part of the eighteenth century. Throughout this period interest was directed towards acquainting an audience of readers with the foreign character of the Romani language.

In the later period, administration and law enforcement officers formed a particular readership for which word lists were published, in an effort to acquaint them with the habits and speech of the Gypsies, as background for enforcing regulations and decrees restricting their movements. It was during the late seventeenth and early eighteenth centuries that research on the Romani language became included in research on the slangs and jargons of thieves and peddlers. While it could be shown that Romani was a separate language that occasionally provided a source of vocabulary items for such jargons and slangs, many people began to regard the two as identical, a misconception still encountered today. Romani is the language of an ethnic group, not a social group.

The discovery of the Indian connection

In the second half of the eighteenth century the grammar and the origin of the Romani language became the subject of intensive scholarly discussion. Its aim was to draw on linguistic evidence in order to determine the origin of the Gypsies. Between 1760 and 1785 various people were engaged in Romani-related research – among them William Marsden and Jacob Bryant in England, the Hungarian Istvan Vali in the Netherlands, Christian Büttner, Johann Rüdiger, and Heinrich Grellmann in Germany, H.L.C. Bacmeister, Simon Pallas and even Catherine the Great in Russia. They discovered, partly in co-operation and partly independently of one another, similarities between Romani and living Indo-Aryan languages of India. Grellmann is usually credited with the discovery of the Indic origin of Romani, probably since he devoted an entire chapter to this topic in his book on Gypsies, a work which was subsequently translated into English and other languages. But it was Rüdiger whose original essay on Romani in fact constituted the breakthrough.

Rüdiger sought the help of a native speaker, a Romani woman of the Sinti group named Barbara Makelin, in obtaining Romani translations of phrases. He compared these translations with Hindustani (Hindi-Urdu of India/Pakistan) and was able to show that the two languages shared not only some basic vocabulary, but also the essentials of grammatical structure. One of the things that caught Rüdiger's attention was the difference in structure where Romani copied the structure of its contact languages. Thus, as early as the late eighteenth century Romani was already providing scholars with insights into the mechanisms of language contact and its effect on language change.

The beginning of modern scholarly research

Work on Romani during the nineteenth century may be said to have centred largely around a comparative investigation of the dialects of the language. Numerous vocabularies, short grammatical descriptions and stories in the

37

The ~~few~~ Welch gypsies mostly call
a pranza lodɜben.

---

manai mɨ **duk** kek fetɜdér
   my   (suggested ? ? ?)
dukɜben   ache. Don't know but—
kai si fɛ duk?
rovela dukasa. I'd rather say "dukasa".
[Has E.W. really heard this word?]
si man duka   (of course if
   you've said pain̲s̲)
lela drab dukeski. (m) he is taking
   medicine for his pain. (Sounds
   all right)
dukavela for head.
kodɜvela for hand, foot. } hurt-ache!

---

x   lias les pesa. he ~~took~~ it with him
     (relative)

Never heard a word for g̲r̲e̲e̲n̲.

If I knew that word I'd have it
   stuffed!
of it on that both ways.

An example of scientific research on language. In the summer of 1894 the Librarian and self-trained linguist John Sampson met the Romani harpist Edward Wood in Wales.

Wood became one of Sampson's sources for his grammar and dictionary of Welsh Romani, published 32 years later, still the most comprehensive grammar of any

sikavela   show : make clear.

šer'la. šeršla . for a long time

x   mižʒmaṣkro silo   he is a dead
             wrong'un. mischief maker

mižʒmaŋgre sò dui.   They're
          both mischiefmakers.

abl. o dui leude si mižʒmaŋgr.

---

kai kesa buti? where are you
      working?

baude kova.   tie that up.

kāshteyge roi   wooden spoon

---

chumʒdas man duvari.
    she kissed me twice.

chumʒdom la.   I kissed her.

chumʒrava la.   I will k. her.

dui chumara.   2 kisses

chindom chuma. sounds ugly.

chumer la   k. her

bâro chumerʒben sas adoi
    don't know if I've heard it — a
    sort of kissing match.

Romani dialect. These notes are some of John Sampson's earliest field notes on Welsh Romani as spoken by Edward Wood. The drawings also show Edward Wood.

language were published. The first efforts to translate texts into Romani emerged, including the first attempt to translate parts of the Bible into Romani. Two works that appeared during this century are of outstanding importance. The first is the comparative investigation of the dialects of Romani, including a comprehensive dictionary, published by the German scholar August Pott in two volumes in 1844-45. Based on the structure of the different dialects, Pott was able to conclude that Romani is a proper language rather than a jargon. He also showed that its dialects represent divergent developments of what would earlier have been a linguistic unity. He further made some significant progress in research into the origins of the language, identifying layers of words of Iranian, Armenian and Greek origin, and further explaining the development of the core Indic component of Romani and its relation to older Indic languages, notably Sanskrit. All this enabled scholars to assume a migration from India, via West Asia, to Europe sometime in the Middle Ages.

The second noteworthy scholarly work is that of the Slovene-Austrian Franz Miklosich. He published a twelve-part series *Speech Varieties and Migrations of the Gypsies of Europe* in which he compared the various dialects, and discussed the particular features of the language as a whole. Based on the way nouns are treated in the language, Miklosich concluded that the ancestors of the Roma must have left India around the tenth century. Miklosich also recognised various layers of lexical borrowings in the language that he regarded as evidence for the migration route which the Gypsies had taken on their way to Europe and for the pathways of different dialects within Europe thereafter. Perhaps his most important observation pertained to the significance of the Greek component. Its presence in all dialects of Romani led Miklosich to conclude that a Greek-speaking area had been the European homeland of all Gypsies before their dispersal across the continent.

The last decade of the nineteenth century also saw the emergence of the *Journal of the Gypsy Lore Society* in Edinburgh as the main forum for scholarly debate and discussion on Romanies in general, and on the Romani language. Contributions included texts in Romani, vocabularies and descriptions of various Romani dialects.

The first three decades of the twentieth century saw yet more significant achievements in the description of single Romani dialects, the most outstanding one being John Sampson's grammar and etymological dictionary of the dialect of the Gypsies of Wales, published in 1926. This work included a detailed description of the development of the sounds and structures of Romani from Indic. It is still an important landmark in the field, especially since it documents a dialect which has since become extinct. During the same period, Romani became to a certain extent included into colonial studies and the discussion surrounding its relations with the languages of subcontinental India as well as with the languages of the Dom and Lom in the Near East thrived.

What do contemporary Romani linguists study?

Modern Romani-related research has since been mostly concerned with the following problems:

1) The unity and diversity of Romani dialects and their implications for both dialect classification and linguistic origins.
2) The impact of language contact on linguistic change, including grammatical borrowing and contact-induced internal innovation, as well as the retention of Romani vocabulary in instances of shift to another language.
3) The sociology of the language, in particular questions of status, codification and standardisation.
4) Romani in the context of current theoretical issues in general linguistics.

A considerable number of linguistic descriptions of individual Romani dialects has been published in the second half of the twentieth century. Since there is no documentation of earlier stages of the Romani language, linguists rely on the comparison of different dialects in their efforts to reconstruct the features of grammar and vocabulary that are common to all dialects thus probably "original" in the language and those that differ and so are more likely to be more recent developments. New evidence on dialects previously unknown to researchers also continues to provide insights into the original grouping of dialects. This in turn might help researchers establish whether there could have already been a division within the speech of the Roma at the time of their earliest settlement in Europe.

Romani is a unique example of a language in contact, since all adult Roma are bilingual, and the language has adopted many items from many different languages. The question of the effect of contact between languages on the individual speaker and on the structure of an individual language has attracted much scholarly attention during the past decades. Students of Romani have had some significant input into the discussion: first, in describing the ways in which Romani may accommodate structures from its contact languages, and, secondly, in describing how Romani input may contribute to the emergence of new speech varieties and jargons which are based on a mixture of Romani words and the language of the respective country. The exact circumstances in which such forms of speech evolve are the topic of ongoing, often controversial, discussion among scholars.

The place of Romani as a minority language in various societies has figured prominently on the agendas of linguists. This pertains especially to the prospects of developing a system of writing, enriching and standardising vocabulary, and developing language resources such as dictionaries, teaching materials and texts. Perhaps the most flourishing of these domains has recently been what linguists call "lexicography" – the compilation of dictionaries. Here, linguists combine two tasks: that of describing Romani dialects for purely scientific purposes, and that of supporting the community of speakers by helping to develop applied resources. In their lexicographic work, linguists have made use of various conventions for writing Romani and have, by doing so, introduced proposals into the discussion surrounding the possibilities of a Romani alphabet – whether a united one or one with variants for each dialect. In addition, linguists have been active participants in the debates surrounding the standardisation of Romani writing, grammar and vocabulary, and much research has been directed towards these efforts.

Further reading

This chapter discusses a number of titles the interested reader can consult in libraries or order through booksellers. Romanestan Publications (22 Northend, Warley, Essex CM14 5LA, England, UK) specialises in books related to Roma, Gypsies and Travellers and in many cases books can be ordered from them by mail. For convenience, we have added ISBN's for those titles which are still available.

Libraries should also be able to provide the books, even if they do not have them in stock, through interlibrary loans.

We have listed books only. There are also many grammatical studies, texts, etc. which are published in scientific journals. They are not listed here but they can be found through bibliographies. A fuller list of recommended publications, covering languages other than English, will be provided in the second volume, with specifications as to region and dialects.

General books

There are many general books on Roma, but not all of them of reliable quality. A solid study of all aspects of the Gypsies is Angus Fraser's book *The Gypsies* (1992). He discusses the history, language and culture, both on a general and country-based level. Jean-Pierre Liégeois's book *Roma, Gypsies and Travellers* (1985, new edition 1994) also gives a good general overview. This book deals not only with Roma, but also with caravan dwellers and other population groups who live or travel in caravans and who are not Gypsies or speakers of Romani. Both books have been translated into many languages.

For those who want to know more, there are also bibliographies which list publications on the subject. Diane Tong's book *Gypsies: a multidisciplinary annotated bibliography* is one of the more recent ones (1995), covering a wide range of subjects with brief comments on all the titles.

As for publications on the language, there are more than one thousand studies, articles, reviews and books devoted to Romani. Not all of these are reliable. A list of these will become available in a bibliography compiled by Peter Bakker and Yaron Matras.

Dictionaries

There is as yet no monolingual Romani dictionary, i.e. one in which the explanations of the Romani words are in Romani. The dictionaries referred to here are translation dictionaries, either from Romani to another language, or from some language to Romani. There are Romani dictionaries for many languages. The following dictionaries are reliable and use English. Full titles can be found at the end of this chapter.

Boretzky and Igla's dictionary of 1994 covers several dialects from Yugoslavia and former Yugoslavia. It is the only multi-dialect dictionary with English translations that is available. It also has an English-to-Romani index. Rade Uhlik's dictionary of 1974 is Serbocroat-Romani-English and also covers several Yugoslav Romani dialects. Vekerdiś dictionnary Romani - Hungarian - English covers several dialects of Hungary. The following dictionaries cover only specific dialects: Demeter and Demeter covers the dialect of the Coppersmiths (Kalderash), as does the vocabulary in Gjerdman and Ljungberg's grammar book. The book by Leksa Manuš and others covers Romani as spoken in Poland, Latvia and other CIS states, and Viljo Koivisto's dictionary is limited to the dialect of Finland. John Sampson's study of the Welsh Romani dialect of 1926 also contains an exhaustive Romani-English dictionary of this variety including comparisons with other dialects.

Apart from these, there are printed Romani dictionaries with translations into Albanian, Bulgarian, Czech, English, Finnish, French, German, Hungarian, Italian, Latvian, Macedonian, Norwegian, Romanian, Russian, Serbocroat, Slovak and probably other languages. Space does not permit a full list but Volume 2 will provide a complete list of dictionaries of Romani into languages other than English.

Grammar books

There are also grammar books on Romani. The following grammars are reliable and written in English. Gjerdman and Ljungberg's *The Language of the Swedish Coppersmith Gipsy Johan Dimitri Taikon* is a comprehensive study of the Kalderash variety as spoken by a Swedish Kalderash storyteller. Ian Hancock wrote a grammar of a general form of Vlax (Kalderash, Lovari, Machvaya) in 1995. Sampson's grammar of Welsh Romani of 1926 (reprinted in 1968) is excellent but no longer in print. Daniel Holzinger published a brief grammar of Sinti in English in 1995 and Petra Cech and Mozes Heinschink wrote a grammar in 1997 of the basket makers dialect of Izmir in Turkey, a variety also spoken in the Balkans.

Some grammars have recently been published in German. We do not give the titles in the list but it is worth mentioning the authors here: Boretzky (1993) describes the Bugurdži dialect of former Yugoslavia, and Boretzky (1994) describes Kalderash; Matras (1994) describes aspects of Kalderash-Lovari, Holzinger (1993) describes Sinti, Igla (1996) a dialect of Athens (Greece), Halwachs (1997) describes the Burgenland dialect. An extensive grammar in French is the one made by Alexandre Paspati in 1870. A reprint from a German publisher is still available. Kepeski and Yusuf (1980) is a grammar written in Romani and Macedonian.

There is no teaching material available in English for Romani, apart from a course by Ronald Lee and edited by Donald Kenrick which was published in the Indian journal *Roma* (Chandigarh) but this is not easy to obtain. Ian Hancock's book *A Handbook of Vlax Romani* is intended for a general audience and could be considered a teaching grammar. There is also a course written in French of the Kalderash dialect by André Barthélémy, for which tapes are also available.

Texts

There are several good books with stories in Romani, made accessible with a translation into English and often with a word list. The most recent one is Lars Gjerde's *The Orange of Love* with Lovari stories from Norway, in the original language and English. The book includes a Lovari vocabulary as well. A number of books with transcriptions of oral stories have been published in Hungary as well, for example the stories recorded by Károly Bari, Grabócz Gábor and others. The stories of the Hungarian Romani story teller János Berki are available in a trilingual Romani-Hungarian-English book, edited by Veronika Görög. Several collections of folk songs with English translations were published by the Hungarian Academy of Sciences, by ethnomusicologists such as Katalin Kovalcsik, Eva Davidová and Ernö Kiraly.

For the *Pogadi Jib* dialect spoken in England, there is a book called *Romani Rokkeripen To-Divvus* containing grammatical studies and texts, edited by Thomas Acton and Donald Kenrick (1984). It is out of print.

Journals relating to Roma

In many countries, Roma have one or more periodicals in which they exchange national and international news, especially that which is relevant for Roma. There are too many titles to list here. There are also a number of scholarly journals which specialise in Roma and Romani. They also publish texts in various dialects of Romani.

We list a number of international journals which specialise in Roma and which also publish regularly articles about the Romani language in English.

Roma. Published in Chandigarh, India. Most of it is in English, some in Romani. Address: Roma Publications, 3290/15-D, Chandigarh 160.015, India.

Interface. Relates to educational issues of Roma, Gypsies and Travellers. This newsletter is free and regularly contains articles relevant for language-related issues. Address: Centre de recherches tsiganes, Université René Descartes, 45 rue des Saints-Pères, 75270 Paris Cedex 06, France.

Romani Studies. Formerly *Journal of the Gypsy Lore Society*. The first issue was published in the nineteenth century in England but since the 1980s it has been published in the United States. It contains articles on Romani and texts in Romani, especially in earlier years. Older issues can be found in larger libraries. Address: GLS, 5607 Greenleaf Road, Cheverly, MD 20785.

Romano Džaniben. Published in Prague, mostly in Czech and Romani, but most articles have summaries in English, French or German as well. Address: Romano Džaniben, Cimburková 23, 130.00 Praha 3, Czech Republic.

Grazer Linguistische Studien. This journal regularly has articles on Romani in English or German, and sometimes special issues on the language. Address: GLS, Institut für Sprachwissenschaft, Merangasse 70, A 8010 Graz, Austria. The Romani-related articles can also be read on their website.

Studii Romani. Bilingual Bulgarian-English. They also publish many texts in Romani. Address: Compl. Emil Markov, bl. 110, entr. 4, app 64, 1404 Sofia, Bulgaria.

List of books mentioned in this chapter

Acton, Thomas and Donald Kenrick. *Romani Rokkeripen ToDivvus. The English Romani Dialect and Its Contemporary Social, Educational and Linguistic Standing.* London: Romanestan Publications, 1984. [ISBN 0 947803 00 9].

Bakker, Peter and Yaron Matras. In preparation. *An indexed bibliography of Romani linguistics.*

Barthélemy, André. n.d. Zanes Romanes? [Course in Kalderash, through French; with tapes].

Boretzky, Norbert and Birgit Igla. *Wörterbuch Romani-Deutsch-Englisch für den Südosteuropäischen Raum.* [Dictionary Romani-German-English for the southeast European area]. Wiesbaden: Harrassowitz, 1994. 418 pp. [ISBN 3-447-03459-9].

Cech, Petra and Mozes Heinschink. *Sepečides Romani.* Unterschleissheim: Lincom Europa. *Languages of the World. Materials,* 1997. [ISBN 389-5860-360].

Davidová, Eva and Jan Zižka. *Folk music of the sedentary Gypsies of Czechoslovakia.* Budapest: Institute for Musicology of the Hungarian Academy for Sciences, 1991. [ISBN 963 7074 30 9].

Demeter, R.S. and P.S. Demeter. *Cygansko-russkij i russko-cyganskij slovar' (kelderarskij dialekt) / Gypsy-English dictionary* (Kalderash Dialect) [Russian-Romani and Romani-Russian Dictionary] (ed. by L.N. Cherenkov). Moskva: Russkij Yazyk, 1990. [ISBN 5-200-00406-3].

Fraser, Angus. 1992. *The Gypsies.* Oxford Blackwell. [ISBN 0-631-15967-3].

Gjerde, Lars. *The Orange of Love and Other Stories. The Rom-Gypsy Language in Norway.* Oslo: Scandinavian University Press, 1994. [ISBN 82-00-41094-3].

Gjerdman, Olof and Erik Ljungberg. *The Language of the Swedish Coppersmith Gipsy Johan Dimitri Taikon.* Uppsala / Copenhagen: Lundequistska Bokhandeln / Ejnar Munksgaard, 1963. [Available in some libraries].

Görög, Veronika (ed.). *Tales of János Berki. Told in Gypsy and Hungarian.* Budapest: MTA Néprajzi Kutató Csoport, 1985. [ISBN 963 7761 93 4].

Grabócz, Gábor and Katalin Kovalcsik (eds.). *Mihály Rostás, a Gypsy Story-Teller.* Budapest: MTA Néprajzi Kutató Csoport, 1988.

Hancock, Ian F. *A Handbook of Vlax Romani.* Columbus, OH: Slavica Publishers, 1995. [ISBN 0-89357-258-6].

Holzinger, Daniel. 1995. *Romanes (Sinte)*. Unterschleissheim: Lincom Europa. *Languages of the World. Materials* LW/M 105. [ISBN 389 5860174].

Kepeski, Krume and Šaip Yusuf. *Romani Gramatika – Romska Gramatika*. Skopje: Naša Kniga, 1980.

Kiralj, Erne [Ernö Kiraly]. *Ernö Kiraly's collection of Gypsy folk music from Voivodina*. Budapest: Institute for Musicology of the Hungarian Academy for Sciences, 1992. [ISBN 963 7074 38 4].

Koivisto, Viljo. *Romano-Finitiko-Angliko Laavesko Liin. Romani-suomi-englanti sanakirja. Romany-Finnish-English dictionary*. Helsinki: Kotimaisten Kielten Tutkimuskeskuksen Julkaisuja 74. Painatuskeskus, 1994. [Finnish Romani dialect] [ISBN 951-37-1363-6] [publisher's address: KKTK, Sörnäisten rantatie 25, FIN 00500 Helsinki, Finland].

Kovalcsik, Katalin. *Vlach Gypsy folk songs in Slovakia*. Budapest: Institute for Musicology of the Hungarian Academy for Sciences, 1985. [ISBN 963 0164 04 3].

Lee, Ronald and Donald Kenrick. *Learn Romani*. Course in Romani, written in English. [Order from: Roma Publications, 3290/15-D, Chandigarh 160.015, India].

Liégeois, Jean-Pierre. *Roma, Gypsies, Travellers. Socio-cultural data. Socio-political data*. Strasbourg: Council for Cultural Cooperation. Strasbourg: Council of Europe Press, 1995. [ISBN 92-871-2349-7].

Manuš, Leksa, Jānis Neiland, Kārlis Rudevič. *Čigānu-Latviešu – Angļu un Latviešu – Čigānu Vārdnīca* [Romani-Latvian-English and Latvian-Romani dictionary]. Riga: Zvaigzne ABC, 1997. [ISBN 9984-04-548-X] [publisher's address: SIA, K. Valdemara ielā 105, Riga, Latvia 1013].

Paspati, Alexandre G. *Etudes sur les Tchinghianés ou Bohémiens de l'Empire Ottoman*. Constantinople: Koroméla, 1870 [reprint 1974, Osnabrück: Biblio/Zeller]. [ISBN 3-7648-0541-2].

Sampson, John. *The Dialect of the Gypsies of Wales*. Oxford: Clarendon Press, 1926. [Reprinted in 1968; out of print; available in some libraries].

Tong, Diane. *Gypsies. A Multidisciplinary Annotated Bibliography*. New York: Garland, 1995. [ISBN 0-8240-754-2].

Vekerdi, Jósef. *A magyarországi cigány nyelvjárások szótára*. [Dictionary of Hungarian Romani dialects; Romani-Hungarian-English]. Pécs: Johannes Pannonius Tudományi egyetem Tanárképzo kar, 1983. *Tanulmányok a cigány gyerekekkel oktatásával foglalkozó munkacsoport vizsgálataibol* VII.

Some Romani websites

Websites are very volatile. We list websites with a (part) Romani content here, but some addresses may have changed location or may no longer be available by the time this book is in print. Also, new websites will have been developed which are not in our list. By searching through the links (which most of them provide) on the available websites it is usually possible to find others of interest. We trust that at least some remain accessible and that these will provide links to sites which have moved in the meantime. For those without access to the Internet, computers in public libraries can usually be used on asking the library staff for assistance.

The list limits itself to sites providing information in or about the Romani language. Many of these websites provide broader information on Roma, for instance on human rights, culture, literature, politics, country-related news, religion, etc.

<http://www2.arnes.si/~eusmith/Romany/index.html> is a website on Romani, listing words, sentences, names, brief sample texts, etc., all taken from a variety of sources – few of them, however, from native speakers or from linguists.

<http://www.geocities.com/Athens/Styx/2105/1.htm>. For people who want to learn some Romani, through English. The person who made this home-page is teaching himself the language by means of song texts, and on this website the user can learn with him. It is the Slovak Romani dialect.

<http://perso.wanadoo.fr/balval/> is a French website, on which one can find brief fragments of music in Romani as well as a poem in Romani by Jan Kochanowski under the heading "révolution", read by the author. There are also numerous other Roma-related items, and a score of links.

<http://home.sol.no/~knutso/romani2.html> contains a text in the Para-Romani language of the Resende of Norway with Norwegian and English versions as well. The website also contains an extensive dictionary of the Para-Romani variety as it is spoken in Norway, with Norwegian and English translations.

<http://w1.422.telia.com/~u42207304/index.htm/> is a similar website of the Resande or Romanimanusj in Sweden. It is in Swedish, English and in their own language. In their guest book there are also letters in their language.

<http://www.dss.unipi.it/intercultura/yusuf.htm> contains a grammatical sketch of the verb in the Arli dialect of Macedonia, written in Italian. It is translated from the Romani grammar (in Romani) by Krume Kepeski and Šaip Yusuf.

<http://shop.logos.it/idiomania/gyp_c.html> contains a text on Romani in Spanish, in which Romani words are compared with Hindi and Sanskrit.

<http://www.radio.cz/romove/lang.html> provides information on the language and its dialect divisions. Texts can be found at <http://www.radio.cz/amaro_gendalos>

<http://www.helsinki.fi/~tasalmin/europe_report.html#Romani> is part of a report on endangered languages in Europe but is not wholly reliable.

<http://www.sil.org/ethnologue/special.html> has some information about Romani but it is incomplete and not always reliable.

<http://www.romani.org/toronto> has a number of song texts in Romani. It is the website of a Canadian Romani organisation, with good information on history, culture, language and human rights.

<http://www.unionromani.org/romani.htm> is the website of a Spanish Romani organisation, with a wide variety of information in Spanish, English and Romani.

<http://www.geocities.com/Paris/5121/glossary.htm> provides a ten page glossary of terms relating to Romani, among them many Romani words.

<www.inbrapenet.com.br/gipsy/>. The Brazilian journalist and audiologist Maria Rosa Wanovich Estevão Abelia has a list of words in her native Kalderash dialect as well as the Calao variety, of which the vocabulary is Romani. This is a form of Brazilian Para-Romani.

<http://sca.lib.liv.ac.uk/collections/gypsy/intro.htm> is the website of the Liverpool library. This library has a huge collection of books, articles, newspaper clippings, letters, photographs, music recordings, etc. relating to Gypsies, Roma and the Romani language.

<http://www.geocities.com/Paris/5121/gelem.htm> contains the Romani text and English translation of the Romani anthem *Gelem, Gelem*. The song can also be heard here, performed by a group called Romale Shavale (this means: "Roma! Boys!")

<http://www.domlang.fi/tutkimus/bibliografia.html> is a list of publications (bibliography) of the Finnish Romani language. There is also additional information on the language at:

<http://www.domlang.fi/tutkimus/romani.html> – but it is in Finnish only.

<http://www.geocities.com/Paris/5121/language.htm> contains solid information about the Romani language. This part of the recommended PATRIN website, carrying a wide range of information regarding Roma. The webmaster is a French-American Rom.

<http://christusrex.org/www1/pater/JPN-r> is the website of a religious organisation which contains many version of the Lord's Prayer and Hail Mary in hundreds of languages. Around a dozen Romani and Para-Romani versions can be found here.

<http://home.sol.no/~pmeek/> is the website of the Norwegian *Romanifolkets landsforening* (national union of Romani people), which contains, among others, song texts in Norwegian Para-Romani.

<http://www.romapage.c3.hu/rovat08/mtilo.htm> contains news items in Lovari. It is part of a Hungarian website devoted to Hungarian Roma.

<www-gewi.kfunigraz.ac.at/romani/>, the website of Austrian Romani-related projects, is probably the best of all concerning Romani. Accessible in German, English and Romani, it carries the texts of periodicals, transcribed oral texts, dictionnaries, bibliographies, articles and a list of Austrian publications on the language. There are written and transcribed, tape-recorded stories and articles in several dialects, notably Burgenland Roman, Kalderash and Lovari.

List of illustrations

p. 51	This song, with music, was the first to be written down in Romani in the 17th century. The meaning of the text is still not completely clear. From: *Codex Caioni s. XVII*. Published by Hungarian Academy of Science, Institute for Musicology, Budapeszt, Hungary, in the series *Musicalia Danubiana*. [ISBN 963-42-0133-6, 963-7074-44-9, 963-7074-45-7].
p. 55	Romani riddles.
p. 70	This map shows the major dialect divisions of Romani according to scholars. Map: Peter Bakker.
pp. 72-73	Drawing by Ferdiand Koçi in *Interface* n° 23, Paris, Centre de recherches tsiganes, August 1996, pp. 14-15.
p. 78	Norwegian Romani or Rommani is one of those rare varieties in which the lexicon is all Romani, but the word endings and structure of the sentence is from another language, here Norwegian. The same text is given in Norwegian and English as well. Source: website http://home.sol.no/~knutso/romani2.html
p. 82	This pamphlet in Romani and Czech was distributed during the velvet revolution in Czechia. Collection: Milena Hübschmannová, Prague.
p. 84	The song "Gelem, Gelem" can be considered the Romani national anthem.
p. 87	The Roma theatre group Romathan from Slovakia and Germany, who perform their plays in the Romani language. Photo by Romathan in *Interface* n° 22, Paris, Centre de recherches tsiganes, May 1996, p. 8.
p. 88	Filmmaker Tony Gatliff made several films in Romani, among them "Gadžo Dilo" and "Latcho Drom". In Lien Social, n° 269, Toulouse, July 1994, p. 25.
pp. 91-94	This letter (pp. 93-94) that a Sinti man had sent to his wife is one of the first published texts of a Romani speaking person. It was published in 1755 in Germany, with a German translation. The first lines mean "My dear wife, I travelled from Frankfurt to Neustadt (the word used in Sinti is the literal translation of the name of this town 'New City'). On my way I had to endure many difficulties ..."
p. 96	This woman, Nada Braidic, won the first price in a Romani poetry contest organised in Italy, in 1994. Photo by Them Romano, in *Interface* n° 17, Paris: Centre de recherches tsiganes, February 1995, p. 21.

p. 97	*O Rukun žal and-i skòla* is one of a few dozen books for children that were produced in Romani. It has been translated from the English book *Spot goes to School.* Paris: Centre de recherches tsiganes / Romani Baxt, 1994.
p. 101	Romani speaking children in a school of Baltëz (Albania) using the ABC-book of the *Interface Collection.* Photo by Ferdinand Koçi.
p. 103	The weekly radio programme of the association "Romano Lil", Paris.
p. 104	Hundreds of Roma all over the world are connected to the Internet. Their correspondence sometimes takes place in Romani.
p. 105	This is the homepage of Patrin on the Internet, which disseminates information about Roma. The introductory text is written in English and in the Vlax and Sinti dialects of Romani.
p. 110	Romani has been written occasionally in Arabic script. This is an example of a part of a word list from Roma in Iran. The first journal produced by Roma was also printed in Arabic script in the 1920's, before Turkey shifted to the use of the western, Roman alphabet. In Dieter Halwachs, *Grazer Linguistische Studien*, n° 46, "Romani I", Graz, 1996, p. 48.
p. 111	Romani has been written in one or two occasions in the Devanagari script of India. Source: John Sampson, *The Dialect of the Gypsies of Wales* (Oxford: Clarendon Press), page of dedication. The study is dedicated to George Borrow.
pp. 114-115	From: *Jekh, duj, trin ... romanes – "Eins, zwei, drei ... auf romanes". Regenbogen-Bücher in Romanes*, p. 16-17. Hamburg: Verlag für pädagogische Medien (vpm), Unnastr. 19, D - 20253 Hamburg, Fax. 49-40-4014711.
p. 117	Many Roma are so poor, that obtaining their daily food is much more important than writing their language. Kalderash in Rome (Italy). Photo by Davide Giangaspero.
pp. 121-123	An example of scientific research on language. In the summer of 1894 the Librarian and self-trained linguist John Sampson met the Romani harpist Edward Wood in Wales. Wood became one of Sampson's sources for his grammar and dictionary of Welsh Romani, published 32 years later and still the most comprehensive grammar of any Romani dialect. These notes

are some of John Sampson's earliest field notes on Welsh Romani as spoken by Edward Wood. The drawings show Edward Wood. Notes published with permission of K. Hooper, University of Liverpool, Gypsy Collections.

The Interface Collection

Interface: a programme

The Gypsy Research Centre at the Université René Descartes, Paris, has been developing cooperation with the European Commission and the Council of Europe since the early 1980s. The Centre's task is to undertake studies and expert work at European level; a significant proportion of its work consists in ensuring the systematic implementation of measures geared towards improving the living conditions of Gypsy communities, especially through the types of action with which it is particularly involved, such as research, training, information, documentation, publication, coordination etc., and in fields which are also areas of research for its own teams: sociology, history, linguistics, social and cultural anthropology...

In order to effectively pursue this work of reflection and of action we have developed a strategy to facilitate the pooling of ideas and initiatives from individuals representing a range of different approaches, to enable all of us to cooperate in an organised, consistent fashion. The working framework we have developed over the years is characterised both by a solidity which lends effective support to activities, and by a flexibility conferring openness and adaptability. This approach, driven by an underlying philosophy outlined in a number of publications, notably the *Interface* newsletter, has become the foundation of our programme of reference.

Interface: a set of teams

A number of international teams play a key role within the programme framework, namely through their work in developing documentation, information, coordination, study and research. With the support of the European Commission, and in connection with the implementation of the Resolution on School Provision for Gypsy and Traveller Children adopted in 1989 by the Ministers of Education of the European Union, working groups on history, language and culture – *the Research Group on European Gypsy History, the Research and Action Group on Romani Linguistics,* and *the European Working Group on Gypsy and Traveller Education* – have already been established, as has a working group developing a Gypsy encyclopaedia. Additional support provided by the Council of Europe enables us to extend some of our work to cover the whole of Europe.

Interface: a network

• these Groups, comprising experienced specialists, are tackling a number of tasks: establishing contact networks linking persons involved in research, developing documentary databases relevant to their fields of interest, working as expert groups advising/collaborating with other teams, organising the production and distribution of teaching materials relevant to their fields;

• these productions, prepared by teams representing a number of different states, are the result of truly international collaboration; the composition of these teams means that they are in a position to be well acquainted with the needs and sensitivities of very different places and to have access to national, and local, achievements of quality which it is important to publicise;

• in order to decentralise activities and to allocate them more equitably, a network of publishers in different states has been formed, to ensure both local input and international distribution.

Interface: a Collection

A Collection was seen as the best response to the pressing demand for teaching materials, recognised and approved by the Ministers of Education in the above-mentioned Resolution adopted at European level, and also in the hope of rectifying the overall dearth of quality materials and in so doing to validate and affirm Gypsy history, language and culture.

Published texts carry the *Interface* label of the Gypsy Research Centre.

- they are conceived as being complementary with each other and with action being undertaken at European level, so as to produce a structured information base: such coherence is important for the general reader, and essential in the pedagogical context;

- they are, for the most part, previously unpublished works, which address essential themes which have been insufficiently explored to date, and because they do so in an original fashion;

- their quality is assured by the fact that all are written by, or in close consultation with, experienced specialists;

- although contributions come from specialists, the Collection is not aimed at specialists: it must be accessible/comprehensible to secondary level students, and by teachers of primary level pupils for classroom use. The authors write clear, well-structured texts, with bibliographical references given as an appendix for readers wishing to undertake a more in-depth study;

- although contributions come from specialists, the Collection is not aimed at any particular target group: in an intercultural approach to education, and given the content of each contribution, every student, and every teacher, should have access to Gypsy/Traveller-related information, and may have occasion to use it in the classroom. The texts on offer, the work of expert contributors, may embody new approaches to the topics covered (history, linguistics etc.) and as such be relevant not only to teachers, teacher trainers, pupils, students and researchers, but also social workers, administrators and policy makers;

- contributions may be accompanied by practical teaching aids or other didactic tools; these tools and materials are prepared by teams in the field, experienced teachers and participants in pilot projects. Their output is very illustrative of *Interface* programme dynamics : an association of diverse partners in a context of action-research, producing coordinated, complementary work, with a scope as broad as Europe, yet adapted to the local cultural and linguistic context;

- format is standardised for maximum reader-friendliness and ease of handling;

- the *Interface* collection is international in scope: most titles are published in a number of languages, to render them accessible to the broadest possible public.

A number of topics have been proposed, of which the following are currently being pursued:

- *European Gypsy history*
- *Life stories*
- *Romani linguistics*
- *Rukun*
- *Reference works*

Jean-Pierre Liégeois
Director of the Interface Collection

Titles in the Interface Collection: a reminder

*The **Interface** Collection is developed by the Gypsy Research Centre at the University René Descartes, Paris, with the support of the European Commission and of the Council of Europe.*

1 • Marcel Kurtiàde
- *Širpustik amare ćhibăqiri* (pupil's book)   CRDP - ISBN: 2-86565-074-X
- Teacher's manual available in: Albanian, English, French, Polish, Romanian, Slovak and Spanish (each with its own ISBN).

2 • Antonio Gómez Alfaro
- *La Gran redada de Gitanos*   PG - ISBN: 84-87347-09-6
- *The Great Gypsy Round-up*   PG - ISBN: 84-87347-12-6
- *La Grande rafle des Gitans*   CRDP - ISBN: 2-86565-083-9
- *La grande retata dei Gitani*   ANICIA/CSZ: 88-900078-2-6
- *Marea prigonire a Rromilor*   EA - ISBN: 973-9216-35-8
- *Die große Razzia gegen die Gitanos*   PA - ISBN: 3-88402-199-0
- *Velký proticikánský zátah*   VUP - ISBN: 80-7067-917-4

3 • Donald Kenrick
- *Gypsies: from India to the Mediterranean*   CRDP - ISBN: 2-86565-082-0
- *Los Gitanos: de la India al Mediterráneo*   PG - ISBN: 84-87347-13-4
- *Les Tsiganes de l'Inde à la Méditerranée*   CRDP - ISBN: 2-86565-081-2
- *Zingari: dall'India al Mediterraneo*   ANICIA/CSZ: 88-900078-1-8
- *Τσιγγάνοι : από τις Ινδίες στη Μεσόγειο*   EK - ISBN: 960-03-1834-4
- *Циганите : от Индия до Средиземно море*   LIT - ISBN: 954-8537-56-7
- *Rromii: din India la Mediterana*   EA - ISBN: 973-9216-36-6
- *Sinti und Roma: Von Indien bis zum Mittelmeer*   PA - ISBN: 3-88402-201-6
- *Ciganos: da Índia ao Mediterrâneo*   SE - ISBN: 972-8339-15-1

4 • Elisa Mª Lopes da Costa
- *Os Ciganos: Fontes bibliográficas em Portugal*   PG - ISBN: 84-87347-11-8

5 • Marielle Danbakli
- *Textes des institutions internationales concernant les Tsiganes*   CRDP - ISBN: 2-86565-098-7
- *On Gypsies: Texts issued by International Institutions* CRDP - ISBN: 2-86565-099-5
- *Текстове на международните институции за циганите*   LIT - ISBN: 954-8537-53-2

6 • Bernard Leblon
- *Gitans et flamenco*   CRDP - ISBN: 2-86565-107-X
- *Gypsies and Flamenco*   UHP - ISBN: 0 900 45859-3
- *Gitani e flamenco*   ANICIA/CSZ: 88-900078-8-5
- *Gitanos und Flamenco*   PA - ISBN: 3-88402-198-2

7 • David Mayall
- *English Gypsies and State Policies*   UHP - ISBN: 0 900 458 64 X

8 • D. Kenrick, G. Puxon
- *Gypsies under the Swastika*   UHP - ISBN: 0 900 458 65 8
- *Gitanos bajo la Cruz Gamada*   PG - ISBN: 84-87347-16-9

- *Gitanos bajo la Cruz Gamada*   PG - ISBN: 84-87347-16-9
- *Les Tsiganes sous l'oppression nazie*   CRDP - ISBN: 2-86565-172-X
- *Хитлеризмът и циганите*   LIT - ISBN: 954-8537-57-5
- *Os Ciganos sob o domínio da suástica*   SE - ISBN: 972-8339-16-X

9 • Giorgio Viaggio
- *Storia degli Zingari in Italia*   ANICIA/CSZ: 88-900078-9-3

10 • D. Kenrick, G. Puxon
- *Bibaxtale Berśa*   PG - ISBN: 84-87347-15-0

11 • Jean-Pierre Liégeois
- *Minorité et scolarité : le parcours tsigane*   CRDP - ISBN: 2-86565-192-4
- *School Provision for Ethnic Minorities:*
  The Gypsy Paradigm   UHP - ISBN: 0 900 458 88 7
- *Minoría y Escolaridad: el Paradigma Gitano*   PG - ISBN: 84-87347-17-7
- *Die schulische Betreuung ethnischer Minderheiten:*
  Das Beispiel der Sinti und Roma   PA - ISBN: 3-88402-200-8

12 • K. Fings, H. Heuß, F. Sparing
- *Von der "Rassenforschung" zu den Lagern*
  Sinti und Roma unter dem Nazi-Regime - 1   ISBN: 3-88402-188-5
- *De la "science raciale" aux camps*
  Les Tsiganes dans la Seconde Guerre mondiale - 1   CRDP - ISBN: 2-86565-186-X
- *From "Race Science" to the Camps*
  The Gypsies during the Second World War - 1   UHP - ISBN: 0 900 458 78 X
- *Dalla "ricerca razziale" ai campi nazisti*
  Gli Zingari nella Seconda Guerra mondiale - 1   ANICIA/CSZ: 88-900078-3-4
- *De la "ştiinţa" rasială la lagărele de exterminare*
  Rromii în perioada regimului nazist - 1   EA - ISBN: 973-9216-68-4
- *De la "ciencia de las razas" a los campos de*
  exterminio Sinti y Romá bajo el Régimen Nazi - 1   PG - ISBN: 84-87347-20-7

13 • Joint authorship
- *In the shadow of the Swastika*
  The Gypsies during the Second World War - 2   UHP - ISBN: 0 900 458 85 2

14 • G. Donzello, B. M. Karpati
- *Un ragazzo zingaro nella mia classe*   ANICIA/CSZ: 88-900078-4-2

15 • A. Gómez Alfaro, E. M. Lopes da Costa, S. Sillers Floate
- *Deportaciones de Gitanos*   PG - ISBN: 84-87347-18-5
- *Ciganos e degredos*   SE - ISBN: 972-8339-24-0

16 • Ilona Lacková
- *A false dawn.*
  My life as a Gypsy woman in Slovakia   UHP - ISBN: 1-902806-00-X
- *Je suis née sous une bonne étoile...*
  Ma vie de femme tsigane en Slovaquie   HA - ISBN: 2-7384-8756-4

17 • Жан-Пиер Лиежоа
- *Роми, Цигани, Чергари*   LIT - ISBN: 954-8537-63-X

20 • Joint authorship
- *Europa se burla del Racismo Antología
  internacional de humor antirracista*   PG - ISBN: 84-87347-23-1
- *L'Europe se moque du racisme,
  Anthologie internationale d'humour antiraciste*
- *Europa pfeift auf den Rassismus,
  Internationale Anthologie des antirassistischen Humors*
- *Europe mocks Racism, International Anthology of Anti-Racist Humour*
- *L'Europa si beffa del Razzismo, Antologia internazionale di umorismo antirazzista*

22 • Елена Марущиакова, Веселин Попов
- *Циганите В Османската империя*   LIT - ISBN: 954-8537-65-6

The Rukun Series:

- *O Rukun ӡal and-i skòla*
  Groupe de recherche et d'action en linguistique romani
  Research and Action Group on Romani Linguistics   RB - ISBN: 2-9507850-1-8
- *Kaj si o Rukun amaro ?*   Idem
  RB - ISBN: 2-9507850-2-6

- *I bari lavenqi pustik e Rukunesqiri*   Idem
- English: *Spot's Big Book of Words* /
  French: *Le grand livre des mots de Spot*   RB - ISBN: 2-9507850-3-4
- Castellano: *El gran libro de las palavras de Rukún*
  Português: *O grande livro das palavras de Rukún*   PG - ISBN: 84-87347-22-3

All orders, whether direct or through a bookshop, should be addressed directly to the relevant publisher. Generally speaking, the publishers will be able to offer discounts for bulk purchase by associations, administrative bodies, schools etc. Inter-publisher agreements should make all titles easily obtainable: for example the English version of *From India to the Mediterranean* can be ordered from UHP, customers in Spain should contact their local supplier, PG, for copies of *Širpustik amare ćhibǎqiri*, etc.

Publishers' addresses:

• **ANICIA**
Via San Francesco a Ripa, 62
I - 00153 Roma

• **CRDP** —
Centre Régional de Documentation
Pédagogique Midi-Pyrénées
3 rue Roquelaine
F - 31069 Toulouse Cedex

• **EA** — Editura Alternative
Casa Presei, Corp. A, Et. 6
Piaţa Presei Libere, 1
RO - 71341 Bucureşti 1

• **EK** — Editions Kastaniotis /
Εκδοσεισ Καστανιωτη
11, Zalogou
GR - 106 78 Athènes

• **HA** — Editions L'Harmattan
5-7, rue de l'Ecole Polytechnique
F - 75005 Paris
  • *distribution in Belgium*
  • *distribution in Canada*
  • *distribution in Switzerland*

• **LIT** — Maison d'Edition Litavra /
за Литавра
BG - 1000 Sofia

• **PA** — Edition Parabolis
Schliemannstraße 23
D - 10437 Berlin

• **PG** — Editorial Presencia Gitana
Valderrodrigo, 76 y 78
E - 28039 Madrid

• **SE** — Entreculturas /
Secretariado Coordenador
dos Programas de Educação Multicultural
Trav. das Terras de Sant'Ana, 15 - 1°
PT - 1250 Lisboa

• **UHP** — University of Hertfordshire
Press
College Lane - Hatfield
UK - Hertfordshire AL10 9AB
  • *distribution in Ireland*
  • *distribution in USA*

• **VUP** — Univerzita Palackého v
Olomouci - Vydavatelství
Palacky University Press
Krížkovského 8
CZ - 771 47 Olomouc

• *distribution for some Rukun titles:*
RB — Rromani Baxt
22, rue du Port
F - 63000 Clermont-Ferrand